D0562293

Playwrights In Profile

CAROL BOLT

Buffalo Jump · Gabe · Red Emma

Playwrights Co·op

Playwrights in Profile: Carol Bolt

copyright © 1976 Carol Bolt

published with assistance from the Canada Council and
the Ontario Arts Council.

Playwrights Co-op
8 York Street, 6th Floor,
Toronto, Ontario
M5J 1R2

The Playwrights Co-op is a non-profit organization created in
1972 by Canadian playwrights to promote and distribute
Canadian plays.

This book was designed by David Robinson, typeset at
B.C. Monthly Typesetting Service, and printed by
the Hunter Rose Company, Toronto.

Photo credits: Cover Arnaud Maggs; Red Emma, Michel Lambeth;
Buffalo Jump, Kitchener-Waterloo Record (University of Guelph
production 1975); Gabe, Robert A. Barnett.

Special thanks to Harry Lane, University of Guelph,
Department of Drama.

First printing: May, 1976
Second printing: September 1977
Third printing: August 1979

All inquiries concerning performing rights, professional or
amateur, readings or any use of this material should be
directed to Great North Agency, 345 Adelaide Street West,
Toronto, Ontario M5V 1R5.

ISBN 0-919834-06-X

Contents

Introduction by Sandra Souchotte   7

    Biographical notes on the author   14
    Cast lists   16

Buffalo Jump   19

    Chronology of events   78

Gabe   81

Red Emma   127

Introduction

Carol Bolt is a playwright surrounded by a hum of platitudes which often make her sound like the Queen bee of Canadian playwriting, with the emphasis on productivity rather than product. But besides being highly industrious, Bolt has also shaped a unique form of social documentary drama which uses factual reference material to gain access to an imaginative Canadian mythology.

These three plays represent only a sampling of the thirteen adult and children's plays completed by Carol Bolt from 1970 to 1975. But they are probably her three most cohesive plays, rich in entertainment and dramatic values, politically inspired but romantically motivated and imbued with a keen, sometimes riotous, sense of social injustice.

Central to *Buffalo Jump* (1972), *Gabe* (1973) and *Red Emma* (1974) is an interest in combining theatrical styles and methods: a fluid interchange of locations loosely defined by props and emotional intensities, quick episodic scene changes, direct audience address, and the use of song to develop action or as a divertissement. This willing exhibition of the theatrical process can also be found in Carol Bolt's approach to children's plays.

Both her adult and children's plays have in common a free-form fluctuation of time, place and space, enhanced by a strong entertainment factor which smooths abrupt or unlikely transitions with song, special lighting changes or the emphasis of a significant prop — the train in *Buffalo Jump* or the banner of anarchy in *Red Emma*. This montage format partly results from re-writing plays in a creative collaboration with the director and actors during the rehearsal period. *Buffalo Jump* (which originated as a revue called *Next Year Country*) and the young people's plays *Cyclone Jack* and *My Best Friend is 12 Feet High* were formed completely in rehearsal. These ongoing transformations of the original material also sift fiction, or rather an imaginative interpretation, into factual details aiming at a conscious redefinition of the time-blurred outlines of historical figures.

Each of the three plays in this collection is built around a real person or persons; *Buffalo Jump* on "Red" Walsh and "Slim" Evans, united for dramatic purposes into the single character Red Evans, *Gabe* on Louis Riel and Gabriel Dumont, and *Red Emma* on Emma Goldman. Even though they contain historical fact, Carol Bolt does not think of her plays as documentaries nor is she necessarily interested in presenting a fair and true picture of events or persons. She has stated that she would rather be interesting than accurate and rather be one-sided than give a well-rounded viewpoint honed to dullness.

Her extrapolations from real person to dramatic persons blend investigative reporting with what might be called creative credibilty — a character develops not necessarily from what *is* true but from what might be true as the playwright understands it. The creation of myth and the re-shaping of myth is more important to Carol Bolt than the documentation of history.

> *Myth is more appealing than fact. It postulates that heroism is possible, that people can be noble and effective and change things. Maybe that's why I'm interested in myth. I think that what we were doing in* Buffalo Jump *was making those characters tragic heroes. And it's possible to do that with Riel and Tom Longboat the central character of* Cyclone Jack *and others.*

Buffalo Jump, a political and social indictment of Canadian society of the thirties, manages to be a less serious work than either *Gabe* or *Red Emma*. The play borrows from the mythology of the old west for its central metaphor, equating the workers' protest march to Ottawa with a herd of buffalo about to be stampeded off a cliff. It has tentative links with the romantic epic mythology of a reform quest headed by a virtuous leader who is prepared to do battle with the demons of the land. But any such association must be seen as overt, satirical and comic rather than subliminal, reverential and grave.

With its explicit breakdown between villains and heroes, the play might have become a modern melodrama were it not for its cut-up, cartoon style which turns it into a pastiche of thirties' films, theatre, social conventions and language. The governing mood of the play is the evocation of nostalgia; a nostalgia that is not only concerned with a general picture of the depression but with such specifically Canadian events as the Estevan riot, the On-to-Ottawa trek and the Regina riot. Just as nostalgia for two heroic men structures the mythology of *Gabe*, so nostalgia for

8

heroic events (or at least potentially heroic events) gives rise in *Buffalo Jump* to a myth rooted in popular idealism — the story of what might have been.

The final version of the play is imprinted with the "collective creation" approach of director Paul Thompson and the actors of Toronto's Theatre Passe Muraille, working in conjunction with Carol Bolt. Theatre Passe Muraille uses social history or social actuality as a foundation for communal folk tales of its own devising. The technique of having each actor research and develop individual vignettes, drawn from a central shared experience, results in plays with an amoeba-like fluidity and growth process. The outcome of such an informal arrangement is that the plays tend to remain an appealing collection of parts rather than to become a unified dramatic whole.

Buffalo Jump has a strong line of action represented by the decision, process and result of going to Ottawa but it is also a colourful montage of theatrical pieces. The tone and texture of the play becomes progressively darker as it becomes clear that the oppressive establishment forces will win. At first R. B. Bennett is depicted as a political cartoon figure spouting speeches which accumulate a dense and glorious assortment of mixed metaphors. In the concluding meeting with the worker delegation his lines are clipped and coldly real.

Before she is through Carol Bolt has utilized most of the agit-prop techniques common to the social issue plays of the thirties, transformed them in the end into a carbon-copy of living guerrilla theatre and stopped off along the way for the mock opera sequence of the Golden episode, where the hungry strikers are fed by townspeople singing arias. One special innovation, however, results directly from the Bolt/Passe Muraille process of making plays — the use of concrete image wherein one short sequence capsulizes the larger, on-going conflict. Implementing the rodeo idea used again in *Gabe*, Bolt constructs a fanciful Calgary Stampede scene in which Red Evans rides a bull called R. B. Bennett, to the accompaniment of typical announcer verbiage.

> *There goes the horn. They're out of the chute. Red is holding on but this Bennett is a lot of bull. He's a tough one, ladies and gentlemen, but Red's a fighter. Oh no, he's thrown. Bennett's turning back at him, ladies and gentlemen. Get out of there, Red. Get moving . . .*

This conversion of political antagonism into a bull wrestling contest conjures up the wider more deadly associations of the 'buffalo jump'; a focus shifting from the individual battle between Evans and Bennett to the mass of workers bucking an entire system.

Throughout the play, each actor assumes several parts, emphasizing caricature or surface mannerism instead of character development. This is a practical method of suggesting greater numbers, manipulating reactions and limiting emotional engagement with a character so that political postures can dominate. Role exchange is supplemented with the comic, anti-naturalistic device of having the strikers carry painted cut-out marchers to give a sense of mass. The real and unreal, caricature and character, stylized theatricality and sombre realism nudge constantly against each other until finally the boundaries of the stage are obliterated and the audience is incorporated into the body of strikers and forced to disperse along with them.

Gabe, with its constant interplay between memory images of Louis Riel and Gabriel Dumont and the reality of their modern namesakes, contains the most overt use of myth. The original Riel and Dumont have been refined by time into spiritual heroes who provide a constant source of romantic inspiration for the contemporary Louis and Gabe, but not productive action.

> *Louis Riel! Was the maddest, smartest, bravest Metis*
> *bastard ever wrote his own treaty. Ever fought for the*
> *rights of his people. For their land. Fought for repre-*
> *sentation.*

Gabriel Dumont is remembered as having equivalent mythic proportions,

> *. . . he was the hero. He was the fellow could have made*
> *it happen. Went to war against paddle wheeling steam*
> *boats and the brand-new Gatling gun. Outnumbered.*
> *And he treated the Canadian army like he was hunting*
> *it for game.*

In spite of these courageous poses, the figures from the past did not achieve either their political ideals or their romantic fantasies, so that the characters Gabe and Louis must function within the context of a failed mythology. The heroics of the old myth have also been vulgarized by the low life clichés of modern day Batoche. There was once a battle at Batoche but now there's a sports day and a camp meeting. Gabe and Louis have just finished jail sentences during which their thinking time was spent "reading classic comic books, true west adventures and junior encyclopedia."

10

And even the invincible comic book heroes, admired by Gabe, are destroyed by Henry's remark that it is the white man who writes the comic books. Louis has been a rodeo hero, a crass reduction of the wilderness adventurer and self-sufficient Metis horseman, but high-living lowered even this precarious status to that of rodeo clown. Louis' infatuation with style and romantic image, reinforced by popular media hype, gives the dim-witted Henry his one perceptive comment of the play. Pulling himself out of the bar after being beaten up by Louis, he shouts, "Goddamn fucking Louis Riel cowboy movie" — a reference which merges the two Riels into one illusionistic, commercial image. But this is the pessimistic side of the failed Canadian myth.

The playwright herself feels that *Gabe* is more positive than negative in outlook and characterization, a quality which stems from the humour and whimsical irony of the play. Although evidence of aimlessness and futility seems pervasive, other details support the playwright's suggestion. Gabe and Louis have a kind of "holy agreement" with the past which gives them a vision of the future.

> *And I don't have to beat you, Henry. Because all of us*
> *half-breeds, we're hunters. We got special knowledge.*
> *Of the future.*

There are two things which might allow Gabe and Louis to survive and win; one is their closeness to nature and another is their exercise of free choice, no matter what the limitations of the decision. Louis beats up Henry and goes to jail with the same sense of righteous martyrdom as his ancestor. Gabe rejects the service station job because it makes him feel like a rodeo clown. Instead he embarks into the bush on a purification rite where he has visions and hears voices speaking of his destiny. Gabe is the man capable of guiding the losers of the world through the wilderness and here the losers of the world, as represented by Henry, are the white men of the world.

> *Even if you knew anything about hunting, fishing,*
> *trapping, anything about the land and how to use it,*
> *you'd be dead in the bush, Henry. You're a city man,*
> *Henry. You can't live by yourself.*

The final irony comes once again from a comic book analogy. Gabe may have had his comic book heroes debunked but he turns Henry, and by implication all stupid white men of limited vision, into a cartoon character from an animal comic book. One man is

11

guided by larger-than-life imaginary heroes but the other does not even achieve human dimension. What really separates these Metis from white, city people and what perhaps offers them salvation is the fact that they have a heritage. In the assimilation of the past, Bolt suggests, lies the potential for a future. Only then is it possible to achieve identity.

Red Emma is more single focussed than the other two plays. This play, dealing with only one part of Emma's story, was written expressly with a Toronto actress, Chapelle Jaffe, in mind. Carol Bolt has already planned an epic sequel which will trace Emma's later life, part of which was spent in Toronto. Although the least concerned with Canadian content, the style and sensibility of *Red Emma* link it closely with *Buffalo Jump* and *Gabe*.

Structurally it too draws upon a fluid intermingling of scenes and juxtaposes caricature with real people. While Emma and her fellow anarchists are portrayed as full-blooded characters, Henry Clay Frick is a stereotype capitalist oppressor and operatic dictator, backed up by a duo of one-dimensional Pinkerton men who might have stepped from a vaudeville routine.

Set in New York of 1890, *Red Emma* glorifies the myth of freedom fighters, "the people and the things they can wish for, the beautiful, radiant things." The clue to an interpretation of *Red Emma* lies in the sub-title, "Queen of the Anarchists." The Emma of this story is a young idealistic woman given to histrionic poses and flamboyant gestures. Bolt was far more interested in Emma the adventuress than Emma the revolutionary. Eschewing the dictates and concerns of political drama, she calls the play a romance, allowing (as in *Gabe*) larger-than-life dreams, the search for grand adventures and a belief in heroism to supercede the intricacies of political argument.

Scenes of potential social realism — the meetings in Sach's Cafe, union hall speeches, the making of a bomb with which to assassinate Frick — are all undercut by songs that stylize the action and accentuate romantic heroic or mock heroic stances. As if inspired by Emma's passionate approach to both life and politics, other characters gradually imitate her fervour and rhetoric. Even the stolid Johann Most brings violets to Emma, falls at her feet when she rejects him and eventually speaks of himself as "King of the Anarchists."

Amidst her youthful presumptions and revolutionary sentiments, one speech of Emma's deserves careful consideration. She makes a confident and convincing declaration for women's emancipation which, more than any other aspect of the play, hints that in the future exploration of Emma Goldman's story there is a mature, vital and significant personality to be developed.

Woman's development, her freedom, her independence must come from and through herself . . . by trying to learn the meaning and substance of life in all its complexities, by freeing herself from the fear of public opinion and public condemnation. Only that will set woman free, will make her a force hitherto unknown in the world, a force for real love, for peace, for harmony — a force of divine fire, of life-giving, a creator of free men and women.

Carol Bolt's first attempt to come to terms with such assumptions began tentatively with *Shelter*, the adult play following *Red Emma*. Dealing with five women, the social rituals of a funeral, wedding and election campaign and one woman's decision to run for office, *Shelter* shields its concerns with comedy. Painful decisions and reactions are given an almost surrealistic stylization, absurdity tops reality and the women tend to be representative types instead of fully developed, deeply felt human beings. The play is sparked with imaginative detail, contains skillful comic moments and effectively satirizes small town Canadian banality and political shenanigans.

Shelter is Carol Bolt's first play constructed from a fictionalized interpretation of her own experience and not historical research. With it, she pushes her free-spirited social investigations and playful character creations into fresh imaginative areas.

Carol Bolt's future contribution to Canadian theatre will undoubtedly shape the fervent idealism, whimsical satire, comic flourishes and social commitment of her past plays into mature new works.

Sandra Souchotte

Sandra Souchotte is a free-lance Toronto writer and broadcaster. She has published threatre articles and critiques in Scene Changes *magazine,* The Toronto Star, This Magazine, Canadian Drama *and the* Canadian Theatre Review *and contributes regular theatre reviews to the CBC radio programme "Off Stage Voices."*

Biographical Notes

Born in Winnipeg, Manitoba, August 25, 1941.

Grew up in Vancouver, graduating from U.B.C. in 1961. Has also lived in Wendigo Mines; Sudbury; McReary; Pioneer; London, England; Doverath, Israel; Montreal, Regina and finally, Toronto.

Married to actor David Bolt; one son, Alexander.

Produced Plays

Daganawida, Toronto Workshop Productions, 1970.
Dir. George Luscombe

Next Year Country, Globe Theatre, Regina, 1971.
Dir. Ken Kramer

Buffalo Jump, Theatre Passe Muraille, Toronto, 1972.
Dir. Paul Thompson

My Best Friend is Twelve Feet High, Young People's Theatre, Toronto, 1972. Dir. Ray Whelan, music by Jane Vasey

Cyclone Jack, Young People's Theatre, 1972.
Dir. Tim Bond, music by Paul Vigna

Gabe, Toronto Free Theatre, 1973.
Dir. Robert Handforth

The Bluebird, Black Box Theatre, Toronto, 1973 (narration only).

Pauline, Theatre Passe Muraille, 1973.
Dir. Paul Thompson

Tangleflags, Young People's Theatre, 1973.
Dir. Ray Whelan, music by Jane Vasey

Red Emma, Toronto Free Theatre, 1974.
Dir. Martin Kinch, music by Phillip Schreibman

Maurice, Young People's Theatre, 1974.
Dir. Tim Bond, music by Paul Vigna

Shelter, Young People's Theatre and the UADA, Toronto, 1974.
Dir. Eric Steiner

Finding Bumble, Young People's Theatre, 1975.
Dir. Tim Bond, music by Paul Vigna

Blue, Young People's Theatre, 1974.
Dir. Tim Bond, music by Paul Vigna

Her plays have also been staged by the St. Lawrence Centre (Toronto), Manitoba Theatre Centre (Winnipeg), Theatre London (London, Ontario), Open Circle Company (Toronto), Alberta Theatre Projects (Calgary), Peterborough Summer Festival (Ontario), Manitoba Theatre Workshop (Winnipeg). University of Guelph, University of Western Ontario, York Theatre (Vancouver).

Buffalo Jump, My Best Friend is Twelve Feet High, Cyclone Jack, Gabe, Tangleflags, Red Emma, Maurice, and *Shelter* were originally published by the Playwrights Co-op in playscript; *Cyclone Jack* has also been published by Simon & Pierre; *Maurice* has also been published in *Performing Arts in Canada. Shelter* will be published in 1976 by Talonbooks.

Film and Television

The film of *Red Emma* directed for the CBC by Martin Kinch and Allan King, was broadcast in January, 1976. Two feature film scripts are now in progress, a romantic comedy loosely based on *Cosi Fan Tutte* and a film about Norman Bethune.

The original version of *Buffalo Jump*, under the title *Next Year Country*, was staged by the Globe Theatre, Regina in 1971, directed by Ken Kramer. This revised and rewritten version of the play was first produced by Theatre Passe Muraille, Toronto, June, 1972, with the following cast:

Anne Anglin	Alice Millar, R.B. Bennett's secretary, Dorothy, Mrs. Mountjoy, etc.
Larry Benedict	Nick Sawchuck, Bible Bill Aberhardt, etc.
Michael Bennett	Ed Staple, Sun Reporter, Mayor of Golden, etc.
Peter Boretski	Red Evans, Garth McRae, etc.
Brenda Darling	Marjorie, Mrs. Merriweather, etc.
Howie Cooper	Peter Lowe, Merle Piston, etc.
Richard Farrell	R.B. Bennett, George Bridges, the Wandering Cook, etc.
Alan Jones	Horvath, Fellow Worker Neilson, Stuart "Paddy" O'Neill, etc.
Gordon May	John Cosgrove, Constable Beaumont, etc.
Miles Potter	Norman Lesker, Richard Martin, etc.
John Smith	Mickey, Wilf Carter, Gerry McGeer, Doc Savage, Sam East, etc.

Directed by Paul Thompson
Set Design by John Boyle
Costumes by Gale Garnett

Gabe was first produced by Toronto Free Theatre on February 14, 1973, with the following cast:

Gabe	Peter Jobin
Louis	Sol Rubinek
Rosie	Brenda Donahue
Vonne	Chapelle Jaffe
Henry	Don MacQuarrie

Directed by Robert Handforth
Set Design by Peter Jobin
Costumes by Miro Kinch

Red Emma, Queen of the Anarchists, was first performed at the Toronto Free Theatre, February 5, 1974, with the following cast:

Emma Goldman	Chapelle Jaffe
Helen Minkin	Diane D'Aquila
Alexander Berkman	Nick Mancuso
Fedya	Jim Henshaw
Henry Clay Frick	William Webster
Kreiderman	Miles Potter
Parks	A.J. Henderson
Johann Most	David Bolt
Piano Player	Phil Schreibman

Directed by Martin Kinch
Designed by Miro Kinch
Music composed by Phil Schreibman

BUFFALO JUMP

Act One

An election rally in Estevan, Saskatchewan. ALICE MILLAR, secretary to R.B. BENNETT, sings.

God save our gracious king
Long live our noble king
God save the king
Send him victorious
Happy and glorious
Long to reign over us
God save the king.

> *After this introduction, R.B. BENNETT appears. The cast, scattered as deeply as practical through the audience, react to BENNETT's speech. Some are for, some against. All are vocal.*

BENNETT: My friends in Estevan, in the warp and woof of the Canadian cloth which is our fine British heritage, our immigrants are the embroidery on our sleeves. We want to roll up those sleeves and get to work.

Our country . . . our country, Canada, plunged into the depths of a great economic depression by unconscionable perversions of our great capitalistic system . . . by profiteers and speculators unchecked in nine years of Liberal Party mismanagement . . .

Mr. King and his Liberal Government are not concerned with the spectre of unemployment which stalks our land.

There are 175,000 men unemployed in this country today. 175,000 families with no captain at the helm. 175,000 frail craft awash in this sea of economic misfortune. Mr. King's message to this fleet is, and I quote from his record in Hansard, April 3, 1930, "I would not give them a five cent piece!" Men and women of Canada, Mr. King's words are a small craft warning.

Mr. King says to the men and women of Canada — and again I quote from his Parliamentary record: "I might be prepared to go to a certain length, possibly, in meeting one or two of the

21

western provinces that have progressive premiers at the heads of their governments, but I would not give a single cent to any Tory Government."

Shame! Betrayal!

We pledge ourselves to stop your betrayal in Ottawa. Nine years of betrayal! It didnt take Judas that long.

We pledge ourselves to foster and support a plan for greater Empire trade. We will set sail for the bright horizons of full employment under that proud Banner, the Union Jack; that same standard, ladies and gentlemen, under which our brave fighting men fought and died in the Great War. With that kind of spirit, that kind of sacrifice, the spirit which is symbolized so perfectly in our brave ensign, we will reach port!

I speak for the Conservative Party in Canada. I sail under that standard and the course I steer is the course of the Conservative Party of Canada.

Ask yourselves, why is the ship of state foundering? Why is it awash? Why is this country so beset by economic storms that its present government in Ottawa can do no more than huddle in the cove of political patronage? Mr. King is not a sailor. The Houses of Parliament are not a naval academy.

I am a sailor.

At this moment, I think that the Dominion of Canada is faced with the greatest crisis of its history. We have the crew; we need the captain. We need the platform of the Conservative Party of Canada. We want to blast our way into the markets of the world.

We want Action! Action! Action!

> *From the tumultuous cheering that follows and at another part of the stage comes a radio announcer's election flash.*

REPORTER: Beep. Beep. Beep. Beep. Beep. Beep. Flash. The results of the 1930 federal election are: Progressive and other Parties, 20 seats, Liberal Party, 87 seats, Conservative Party, 138 seats. The Conservative Party led by R. B. Bennett have elected 138 seats and will form the next government.

> *The cast may still be making its way through the audience to the stage. Everybody sings.*

CHORUS:
Looks to me we should all agree
What we need for the people is the farm relief
Looks to me we should all agree
What we need for the people is the farm relief.

SOLO:
Grasshoppers eating up all my grain
Dust blowing round, ain't got no rain
We got good people and it's their belief
What we need for the people is farm relief.

CHORUS:
Looks to me we should all agree
What we need for the people is the farm relief
Looks to me we should all agree
What we need for the people is the farm relief.

> *During the chorus, two of the company move into position to play the following scene. One of them holds a rope knotted into a lariat.*

FARMER: Well, most of what I planted last spring has blown all the way down to Montana and most of the topsoil followed it down. Kind of strange the way a dust storm comes up.

> *The rope begins to swing and continues faster and faster, creating the sound of wind.*

You look up and the sun is kind of hazing over, the wind is whipping up, everything on the farm, except the mortgage, is just blowing past you, out of sight . . .

> *The cowboy throws the rope over the FARMER's shoulders. For the rest of the scene, he circles him, slowly, keeping him at the end of the rope, getting him more and more entangled in the rope and finally bringing him to his knees.*

Well, the best thing to do when that happens is to get your neckerchief up over your mouth and nose, or get inside, but sometimes you can't do that because you're on your way into town for food or you're getting the kids from school.

> *The FARMER sinks to the floor in a coughing, choking fit as the rope wraps him tighter and tighter. At last, the cowboy drops the rope. The FARMER looks up, brightens.*

But this is good country, though. My daddy got fifteen good crops out of this land and I figure everything's going to be all right, just as soon as all this blows over.

CHORUS:
Looks to me we should all agree
What we need for the people is the farm relief
Looks to me we should all agree
What we need for the people is the farm relief.

SOLO:
Children all ragged and they got no shoes
And all we got is the farm relief blues
Us poor people got to work and fret
Cause the doggone farm relief hasn't helped yet.

CHORUS:
Looks to me we should all agree
What we need for the people is the farm relief
Looks to me we should all agree
What we need for the people is the farm relief.

During the chorus, two of the company move into positions to play the following scene.

LESTER: I've been working on it, Howard, I know the farm hasn't been doing very well these last two years, but I've been doing some reading . . .
HOWARD: I've given you two extensions already, Lester.
LESTER: Yes, but I can make something out of it this year. I can get a crop out of her. That's good land, Howard, you know it . . .
HOWARD: Took over three farms in your section just last week. All of them useless.
LESTER: You're not going to take my farm?
HOWARD: I've got your file right here, Lester . . .
LESTER: I need another extension, Howard . . .
HOWARD: I got a letter in here from the head office in Montreal, they want to know why I gave you those first two extensions . . .
LESTER: Goddamn it, Howard, that farm's all I've got.
HOWARD: I got no answer for them . . .
LESTER: I don't know anybody in Montreal. I know you, Howard. Goddamn it, you can't take my farm.
HOWARD: Goddamn it, there's nothing else I can do. I just want you to know, Lester, you're going this week and I'm going next week, this bank's got nothing but equity in land that's worth nothing . . .

24

LESTER: You're going to take my farm?
HOWARD: I'm sorry, Lester, I just can't help you.
LESTER: All right. All right. If that's the way you want it . . .
If that's the way you want it, I guess I'm just going to have to
beg you. *(He sinks to his knees)* Sweet Jesus, don't take my
farm!

CHORUS:
Looks to me we should all agree
What we need for the people is the farm relief
Looks to me we should all agree
What we need for the people is the farm relief.

SOLO:
Freight rates too high and the market's too low
We ask for credit and they all say no
All start working at the break of day
But we got no wheat so we got no pay.

CHORUS:
Looks to me we should all agree
What we need for the people is the farm relief
Looks to me we should all agree
What we need for the people is the farm relief.

> *During the chorus, JOSEPH moves out of the
> group to begin packing. As the chorus ends, his
> FATHER approaches him.*

FATHER: Joseph, I know we're going to be able to plant that
bottom land, down by the slough. And if we send the livestock
to pasture in Manitoba, if we send the cattle, then we'll have
enough feed for old Tom. We couldn't send him, the horses
don't do well away from home, but with the cattle gone,
there'd be enough feed to get him fattened up, get him strong
enough for spring ploughing . . .

> *During his speech, he enters JOSEPH's room,
> notices and realizes that his son is leaving. He
> decides not to mention it, to continue with his
> plans, but at last he trails off.*

JOSEPH: I can't tell you anything about farming, Pa. You
taught me, but I can't stay here any longer, that's all.
FATHER: Where are you going?
JOSEPH: Up north of P.A. There's crops there and there's
timber.

FATHER: You're not a lumberjack.

JOSEPH: I can be.

FATHER: You can work your own land. You're not some-body's hired hand, Joseph, all this land is yours. Your mother and I spent all our lives building up this farm.

JOSEPH: You don't have a farm, Pa. You haven't had a crop for three years.

FATHER: Next year, things will be . . .

JOSEPH: I'm getting out of next year country.

FATHER: You're all I got left, Joseph.

JOSEPH: You don't need an extra hand, for that bottom land, Pa. I don't want to spend a year mending fences. I'm going to make some money, I'm going to save enough to come back and put this farm back on it's feet, run it the way it should be run . . . *(JOSEPH realizes his own dreams are pretty weak)* I'm sorry, Pa. *(He puts his hand on his FATHER's shoulder)*

CHORUS:
Looks to me we should all agree
What we need for the people is the farm relief
Looks to me we should all agree
What we need for the people is the farm relief.

FATHER:
Sitting here watching my farm blow away
Maybe it's in Ottawa, I can't say
If you get there before I do
And there ain't no dust storms, I'll come too.

CHORUS:
Looks to me we should all agree
What we need for the people is the farm relief
Looks to me we should all agree
What we need for the people is the farm relief.

On HORVATH's speech, which is heard from the back or side of the auditorium, the farm relief grouping changes into Mara Lake Relief Camp.

HORVATH: Okay, boys, I want you to take that rock and pound the shit out of it. I want to see gravel!

Everyone in the work camp has heard this speech before. They can sing along. NORMAN has discovered the task for the day is moving boulders from A to B. Everyone else is sitting around.

26

NICK: Going to tell us times are getting better, Norman!

ED: He already said that.

MICKEY: That's the rock we shifted yesterday. He's moving it back where we got it.

NORMAN: This is different rock.

PETE: *(To MICKEY)*   I got a letter from my mother.

MICKEY: Oh, good. That's good. So what, kid?

PETE: If I don't give you the buck I owe you right now, I can send her three dollars.

HORVATH: *(Approaching)*   All right, boys, you finished assing around?

BRIDGES: Oh, Jeez, it's Horvath.

ED: Keep your drawers on, Bridges.

MICKEY: *(To PETE)*   You're playing poker with your little old lady's money?

PETE: You dealt me in.

HORVATH: I want you to try a little harder for me, boys. I want you hustling.

COSGROVE: Government paying you twenty cents a day. Let's show them they're getting their money's worth.

HORVATH: Let's just do that.

>   *All of the men begin to move rock with varying*
>   *degrees of enthusiasm. In addition, COSGROVE baits*
>   *HORVATH with a lot of enthusiasm.*

MICKEY: Listen kid, you don't play poker with your mother's money. You got to have money to lose. Give me my buck.

COSGROVE: I hear R.B. Bennett's coming out to the camps.

HORVATH: What?

ALL: He's unemployed!

COSGROVE: He's sure not doing much.

MICKEY: I wonder what that fine young lady's doing right now. What time is it in Fort William anyway? I guess it's about three hours from now . . .

HORVATH: Some people in Ottawa . . .

COSGROVE: Are a hell of a lot fatter than most people here.

HORVATH: Some people in Ottawa say that relief camps are just a breeding ground for political unrest.

COSGROVE: Just a hot-bed.

MICKEY: So I guess she's helping her mother with one of those fine dinners . . .

ED: *(To MICKEY)*   Standing around doing bugger all.

MICKEY: When I want a job buggered up, I'll ask you in to bugger around.

BRIDGES: That's buggered it.

HORVATH: *(To COSGROVE)* I don't want any trouble.
NICK: Horvath, you got this camp running like a railway watch.
HORVATH: If we do have any trouble, we can bring the bulls in.
COSGROVE: Yes, sirree.
NORMAN: There's a science to it.
BRIDGES: To what?
NORMAN: Lugging boulders.
NICK: Hoo-bloody-rah.
HORVATH: This camp's set up so certain young men can do an honest day's work for their keep . . . and a certain small stipend.
COSGROVE: Twenty cents a day. Why don't you say? Because it's slave labour.
HORVATH: Certain others, in the pay of foreign governments, are bound to take advantage.
PETE: *(To HORVATH)* My mother says she hopes I'm getting lots of exercise.
COSGROVE: *(To HORVATH)* You keep looking for Communists. This relief camp is the best thing that's happened to Communism since Karl Marx.
HORVATH: You don't like it, you can get out.
MICKEY: I like it fine, Horvath. I haven't had such a good time since the Oddfellows took me to the circus.
HORVATH: I got other crews to check on.

RED EVANS has arrived. He is watching the proceedings.

COSGROVE: You want to see a Communist agitator, Horvath? A real one?
HORVATH: *(To another crew, off)* You men, there. You're building a roadbed, not a fucking monument.
COSGROVE: You want to find out what it is you're so afraid of?
HORVATH: *(Leaving)* Come on, come on. You've left your daddy's farm, my friends. You're here to work.
EVANS: *(Handing out leaflets to the men)* My name's Red Evans. I'm a travelling salesman.
MICKEY: *(Looking at his leaflet)* You've come to the wrong place.
EVANS: I sell young Canadian men to Moscow. It's all for the glory of the hammer, the sickle and the international Communist conspiracy.
NORMAN: *(He and MICKEY leave the group)* I knew it.
EVANS: There's a story in this month's issue of your camp paper. Says you men are complaining about the food in this camp.
NICK: Just the ones who like to eat.
EVANS: You know what the government says about that? The food's fine, boys. You got cream of wheat for breakfast, hot cakes and syrup.

28

NORMAN: Just like home.

MICHAEL: It's pig slop.

EVANS: You boys are trouble-makers.

MICKEY: We're in trouble, you Bolshevik bastard.

EVANS: *(Ignoring MICKEY)* You're in trouble. You know why you're in trouble? If you've got grievances, if you want to organize, you can't do it, you're one man, you're a trouble-maker, the government brings in the bulls. Your friend Cosgrove here tells me you had the town bulls in here last week . . .

BRIDGES: Breaking up a poker game.

ED: Mickey there went haywire.

NICK: Ain't the way I heard it.

ED: Just a jack-knife carpenter, fucked and far from home.

MICKEY: I was drunk.

PETE: Man's got a right to be drunk.

MICKEY: I was really drunk.

NICK: On twenty cents a day?

NORMAN: Sawchuck, you're crazy, come on . . .

COSGROVE: Red Evans came all the way up here from Princeton, least you can do is listen to him, honest to Pete . . .

EVANS: You men know about the Relief Camp Worker's Union. We're working for you. We've been working in Vancouver all winter. We've been going into camps to find out what you want, we've been talking to people who are willing to listen to you. You want a decent wage, you want work that means something. There are people in Vancouver who understand that.

NORMAN: Yeah, Reds.

BRIDGES: I don't know . . .

EVANS: They're your people. They're like your folks back home. We got a family in Vancouver that's going to work for you. For decent wages, for a chance to build something that means something. This is rich country boys, we're all part of it. We're going to give you a chance to be part of it again.

NICK: You boys happy here? You like sweating your balls off for twenty cents a day?

PETE: No!

NORMAN: Nick . . .!

MICKEY: The thing I hate about all this union shit is all the stupid questions.

BRIDGES: What else is there?

MICKEY: That's another stupid question.

EVANS: The government wants to keep you in these camps, boys. They want you where you can't find out what your friends are doing, they want to force you into slave labor in a god-forsaken corner of God's country where the people of Canada can forget what's happening to you.

PETE: He's right. Goddamn it, he's right.

NICK: Sure he's right. I'm fed up to here.

EVANS: The Defense Department tells you it's not going to listen to you. The people of Canada, that's your friends and your families, they'll listen. We're going to the people.

BRIDGES: How?

ED: Where?

EVANS: We're going to Vancouver.

NICK: I'm going to Vancouver.

NORMAN: *(To NICK, as he carries him back to the rock pile)* You're not going anywhere, you crazy bastard.

MICKEY: Last time I was in Vancouver, the railway bulls beat my head in.

EVANS: We're going on strike.

PETE: I'm going to Vancouver.

EVANS: Atta boy! It's April 2nd, right? You got paid yesterday. Twenty cents a day for a month. Your friends in Vancouver are going to help you along. There's nothing to stop us, we're going to move.

NICK: *(Lugging NORMAN back)* I'm walking out of here and you're coming with me.

MICKEY: I'm not listening to this shit.

COSGROVE: What about your shit?

MICKEY: I eat it. That's been going on for years.

NORMAN: *(Pushing NICK back)* Sawchuck, there is something gone wrong with your head!

BRIDGES: This could get us in a lot of trouble . . .

COSGROVE: This guy's the best friend you're ever going to have . . .

MICKEY: You go to Vancouver with him, you're going to march down the street in front of him, give the cops something to shoot at.

EVANS: We're going to Vancouver.

NICK: *(To NORMAN)* There's nothing wrong with me, my friend, I've just been here too long. Are you coming with me, Ed?

ED: Sure. Why not? I said I was.

MICKEY: Stupid bastard.

EVANS: Fifty cents an hour. Work that's important.

MICKEY: No one's going to listen to you. Nothing's going to happen.

BRIDGES: Nothing's happening here.

NICK: We'll go to Vancouver. We'll win this one for Mickey. We'll tell them all about the boys we left behind.

MICKEY: Fuck you.

COSGROVE is organizing everyone who is going. He has a real live wire in PETE LOWE.

COSGROVE: All right, why are we going to Vancouver?
(No reply)   That's right . . . work. What else do we want?
PETE: Money! Money!
COSGROVE: That's right, wages! You're a real live wire, aren't you Pete?
PETE: Wait till my mother hears about this.
COSGROVE: *(Making a chant, which the others join)*   We want work and wages. We want. Work and wages. We want. Work and and wages.

> *NORMAN, watching the departing group, throws his hat to the floor in frustration.*

NORMAN: Ah, Jeez, Nick!

> *Someone in the group hits the first note of "LAND OF HOPE AND GLORY." The group, joined by MICKEY and NORMAN, wheel into a kind of cadet chorus line, their caps under their arms. They sing:*

Land of hope and glory
Mother of the free
How shall we extoll thee
Who are born of thee
Wider still and wider
Shall thy bounds be set
God who made thee mighty
Make thee mightier yet
God who made thee mighty
Make thee mightier yet.

> *R.B. BENNETT enters the Imperial Conference. "LAND OF HOPE AND GLORY" is his favourite song so the choir hums the chorus through again. During the hum, BENNETT begins to speak.*

BENNETT: It is a proud day for Canada, for in its capital city are gathered delegates from throughout the empire, empowered to speak for one quarter of the earth's population and instructed to co-operate in delivering a plan by which this great empire may continue its leadership among nations.

I cast my mind back to the beginning of this conference and the dedication service in the Memorial Chapel here in the Houses of Parliament. That chamber commemorates Canada's part in the

Great War. The names of 68,000 of her glorious dead are recorded within those walls. They are only a part of the vast army of our Imperial dead. When that altar was dedicated, in 1927, the then Premier of England, who was present then, as now, made a striking address. He quoted Socrates before his judges: "Now we go our ways. I to die and you to live. But which is better, God only knows."

Now we are sure it is better to live. *(To the choir)* Thank you, boys.

They file off.

Who could see the brilliant assemblage gathered here in Ottawa without flushing, swelling with pride? This company of noble men of splendid purpose is a fresh breeze in the storm of economic ills which sweeps and eddies over all the nations. These fresh breezes will lead us to a cloudless day, smooth sailing, fair winds. The great brotherhood of nations which is the Commonwealth will breathe freely, bask in the sun. The Dominions . . .

The rest of the cast, representing Commonwealth delegates, begin to harass BENNETT and interrupt his speech.

FREE STATE: The Dominions and the Irish Free State.
BENNETT: The Dominions, tied to the mother country by that sterling and sovereign example of brotherhood, our sacred trust, the British Commonwealth of Nations . . .
FREE STATE: The Irish Free State will not bargain with the British oppressor. We object.
BENNETT: We shall see Jerusalem, the Scripture has it. Truly the light is sweet and a pleasant thing it is for the eyes to behold the sun, the Scripture has it. For lo, the winter is past, the rain is over and gone, the flowers appear on the earth and the time of the singing of birds is come, the Scripture has it.
STRAITS SETTLEMENT: Straits Settlement objects to Scriptural references on behalf of our Moslem minority.
BENNETT: We meet in days when the machinery of world commerce is out of gear. International finance has broken down. But we meet in the knowledge that the tools we need to start those wheels moving again are in our hands. I speak of the retention of preferential tariffs.
BALDWIN: I had thought that we would lower tariffs.
BENNETT: Oh, I speak of new preferential tariffs in some areas and I speak of the extension of the free list so that members of the Commonwealth can blast their ways into the markets of the world.

Our Commonwealth ties are an obligation and a sacred trust. Britain buys too much wheat from Russia. She buys from Soviet sources, 21 per cent of her wheat, 32 per cent of her soft sawn woods and 34 per cent of her pit props.

BALDWIN: Russian prices are lower.

BENNETT *(Takes harassment and criticism very poorly)* The question of world trade is a very complicated one. If there were only one view, this conference would not be necessary. I think we can agree, however, that there is only one correct view, one course to steer which will give a stronger, clearer impulse to the life of the whole world. I will try to explain it to you, but you won't understand. You wouldn't understand, even if you understood.

CHATTERJEE: Our basic difficulty was Mr. Bennett's personality.

RUNCIMAN: He has the manners of a Chicago policeman and the temperament of a film star.

> *They leave. During MR. BENNETT's recitation, the stage is cleared of everything except his faithful secretary, ALICE MILLAR.*

BENNETT: In the words of Kipling, that great Empire poet:

If you can talk with crowds and keep your virtue
Or walk with kings, nor lose the common touch
If neither foes nor loving friends can hurt you
If all men count with you, but none too much
If you can fill the unforgiving minute
With 60 seconds worth of distance run
Yours is the earth and everything that's in it
And — what is more — you'll be a man, my son.

> *In another area of the stage, COSGROVE is addressing his boys, who are scattered through the audience.*

COSGROVE: You boys are probably wondering why we're marching so much. It's because we look good. We could stay in the union halls, playing cards all day. But there wouldn't be any point to it. When we're marching around Vancouver, people can see us, they'll keep thinking on why we're here.

Just one thing we can do is learn to march a little better. And the reason for that is probably some people think we've got no pride in ourselves, we're beaten. And if we're marching and it's orderly, we'll look proud. There's a thousand of us down here in Vancouver now, that's going to look pretty impressive. We're asking for work and wages so let's let people know we deserve them.

Okay, let's do some practising.

The boys struggle up, although PETE LOWE is still enthusiastic.

Sure . . . Pete looks good. Doc, Nick, Norman . . . good to see you Norman. Garth looks cock-eyed but there's nothing we can do about that.

Okay. By the left. Quick march! That's good, that looks good, boys. Mr. Hold-the-Fort, give us a song.

The men sing.

CHORUS:
Hold the fort for we are coming
Union men be strong
Side by side we battle onward
Victory will come

We meet today in freedom's cause
And raise our voices high
We join your hands in union strong
To battle or to die

REPEAT CHORUS

Look my comrades see the union
Banners waving high
Reinforcements now appearing
Victory is nigh.

> *By the end of the song, the tempo has been slowed down to a painful halt. At random intervals through the song, the marching formation is frozen, one man steps out of the group and we listen to his "mind-track." For example:*

PETE: Cosgrove, I kind of like all this marching and the people waving back at us, but I got a letter from my mother and I don't know if she's going to be so happy because she thought I was looking for work down here, Cosgrove and I . . .
O'NEILL: . . . Going to listen. They can't help it. Fifteen hundred men down here and all yelling "Work and Wages!" And the people are all yelling back . . .
BRIDGES: Never going to remember the words of that damn song. "See our banner still approaching" . . . how the hell does it go?
ED: . . . don't know about these fellows but I got a stone in my shoe. But apart from that, everything's wonderful, sure, only problem is we're marching and my left foot keeps hitting the god-fearing blue-assed ground . . .

On another stage area, a spotlight, definitely a special, comes up on WILF CARTER.

WILF: Hi folks, I'm Wilf Carter.

I know you all remember the men who made the Calgary Stampede great, names like Herman Linder, Clem Gardner, Pete Knight. They were all roping experts and bronco-busting champions.

As long as we remember those men, and as long as the golden poppies are blooming 'round the shores of Lake Louise, I'm proud to be a Canadian and I'm going to sing a little song:

The trail to that last happy round-up
Is narrow and steep so they say
But the broad one that leads to perdition
Is posted and blazed all the way

It's roll on, little dogies roll on
Roll on little dogies, keep rolling along
Roll on, little dogies, roll on
Roll on, little dogies, roll on

YODEL

Roll, little dogies, roll
Roll you little dogies keep rolling along
Roll, little dogies, roll,
It's roll, little dogies, roll.

And the lights fade down.

COSGROVE: *(From the back of the hall)* Company dismissed!

Loud cheers. NORMAN, NICK, ED and GARTH race for the stage.

NORMAN: We got four hours off.
ED: Four hours. No meetings, no marching, no boxcars.
NORMAN: Jesus, look at that. That guy's got a dozen or more relief camp sweaters sitting in that window. Those deadheads are selling their sweaters.
ED: They'll freeze their asses off.
NORMAN: Wonder who thought of that.
NICK: Smell that ocean.

The ocean smells more like the docks today. NICK, NORMAN and ED don't mind. GARTH is not so sure.

ED: What are we going to do?
GARTH: We're going up to Pender Street. Chinatown. Good place for a good time if you know the right places. Fan tan games. Opium dens. Won ton duck.
ED: All we've got are meal vouchers.
GARTH: Tong wars.
ED: Say, you think they'd take meal vouchers?
GARTH: By Jesus, I got a relief camp sweater, there's a fellow in that store back there going to want it for his collection.
NICK: You can't do that, Garth.
GARTH: Get me enough for a couple of beer.
NORMAN: You can't do that, Garth. Hang around a beer parlour.
NICK: Make us all look bad.
GARTH: I was talking to Evans . . .
ED: Sure you were.
GARTH: He asked me to be a group leader. Said I had natural ability.
NICK: Oh, sure.
GARTH: As a matter of fact, I told Evans he's got this trek organized all wrong. We're acting too quiet. What we want to do is raise a little hell.
ED: What did he say to that?
GARTH: I told him that in my experience, many of your enquiring minds in town will congregate in your hotel beverage room. I told him I'd be willing to take our message to those folks.
NICK: What did he say to that?
GARTH: You're a cattleman, he says to me. That's right, I says, and we know what that means. Takes something to head spooked cattle in a thunder-storm, break a bronco. You're a veteran, he says to me, you've seen battle.
NICK: Thought you were tying your shoe-lace just as the army left.
GARTH: I'm a veteran. I was wounded. I'm a pensioner.
ED: You know what I'd like? There'd be a girl, walking down the street here. A really pretty young girl, maybe still in high school and we'd stop to talk to her and we'd walk down to the ocean with her and just look out over the water and we'd talk . . .
NORMAN: And maybe she'd have a friend.
NICK: You go down to the waterfront here, the longshoremen have just walked out.
GARTH: Never found myself a really pretty girl. All my women built more for speed than for style.
NICK: We should be on that picket line.
NORMAN: Jesus, Nick, we're in Vancouver.
NICK: I know. And there's a walk-out.
ED: We've only got four hours off.

36

NORMAN: Look, I followed you down here from the camps, right? I haven't been past Vancouver railway yards and the relief camp office unless I'm marching in a line . . .

NICK: We've got no money, we've got no place to go. Let's do something useful. Get in a little excitement.

NORMAN: No.

NICK: No?

NORMAN: You heard me.

NICK: What do you mean, no?

NORMAN: I've been in the camps with you. I've been marching around Vancouver with you. And now I've got four hours off.

NICK: And we can go down to the docks . . .

NORMAN: Red said we should have some fun.

NICK: Okay, let's go and break the bank at Monte Carlo.

ED: I was stooking wheat last summer. I ended up in Winnipeg. I was walking down Lumbard Street, past the Y.W.C.A. . . . .

NICK: *(He is somewhat more sophisticated)* The Y.W.C.A., Jesus!

NORMAN: Church. Girls go to church.

ED: There was this girl. I guess I wasn't watching where I was going and I bumped right into her. She was carrying a lot of parcels and I knocked them all over the street.

NICK: You are so stupid, Ed . . .

ED: But she didn't mind. I helped her pick up the parcels, she was laughing . . .

> *Two girls who have been watching the boys laugh. There is a standoff. The girls are pretending they are not watching the boys, the boys are trying to decide what to do.*

ED: Jesus, look at that.

NORMAN: *(To NICK)* Now, that's Vancouver.

ED: What are they doing standing around the street corner?

NORMAN: They're waiting for a streetcar.

ED: Say something.

NORMAN: You say something, Nick.

NICK: Tell her you want to carry her packages.

> *NICK pushes NORMAN over to the girls. He is nonplussed.*

NORMAN: You girls go to church?

NICK: Oh, Jesus.

> *The girls giggle. MARJORIE, who takes a while to wind up, pushes DOROTHY forward.*

37

DOROTHY: You're from the relief camps, aren't you?
NORMAN: Yes, I'm a Methodist.
DOROTHY: You're wearing a sweater just like all the other fellows we see walking . . .
NORMAN: I mean, we're from the relief camps.
MARJORIE: *(To DOROTHY)* I told you.
DOROTHY: You're out on strike.
NORMAN: Well, we're down here in Vancouver. I guess you girls know Vancouver . . .
ED: *(Who has edged over to join the group)* What there is to do in this town . . . we've got four hours off.
NORMAN: Where this streetcar goes, for example.
DOROTHY: East on Hastings past the exhibition grounds.
NORMAN: Oh good, the exhibition grounds. That's probably something to see.
DOROTHY: We're going home.
NORMAN: Oh?

> *There is another standoff. The girls turn away but the boys are still standing there. DOROTHY finally takes pity on them.*

DOROTHY: What's it like in the relief camps?
MARJORIE: My father says you boys are doing a fine brave thing. He says that only the people are going to set this country back on its feet and it's time that the people got together to protest and organize. My father voted for Angus McInnis in the last election and he says the days of the two old parties are past.
DOROTHY: What's it like in the relief camps?
NORMAN: It's rough.
MARJORIE: My father says it's just like a forced labour camp. My father says the government set them up so all the young men would be out of the cities, so that the capitalists could just make people believe that times weren't as bad as they are. My father says the capitalists are expecting armed insurrection and riots in the streets and they should be, the way they're exploiting the people. My father says there is no wealth, wealth is just a way of dividing people against each other in the class war. Wealth is just a product of our labour.
GARTH: Say, that little girl is making me thirsty.
DOROTHY: Who's that?
ED: Oh, that's Garth McRae.
NORMAN: Garth says he has a meeting with Red Evans. See you later, Garth.
GARTH: Say, I first came out west with the railway. I opened up the territory. *(No response from the boys)* Ended up hanging

around a bunch of green kids. Acting coltish. *(Still nothing)*
Well, hold the fort, boys.

> *GARTH leaves.*

DOROTHY: Is Mr. McRae one of your organizers?
NICK: *(To DOROTHY)* No, Norman here, he's the organizer.
DOROTHY: Have you been in politics long, Mr. . . . ?
NORMAN: Politics?
MARJORIE: He's from the relief camps, dodo. He's devoted
himself to the class struggle.
NORMAN: Yes.
NICK: His whole life is the worker's cause.
NORMAN: Work and wages.
NICK: He wants to go down to the docks, join the longshore-
men's walk-out.
DOROTHY: I think that's wonderful.
NORMAN: But we don't have to do that now.
DOROTHY: Oh, no, we wouldn't want to keep you.
NORMAN: Oh, no, it isn't that, no, you could help us.
ED: You could walk down to the docks with us.
DOROTHY: *(To ED)* We couldn't do that.
ED: Why not?
DOROTHY: We'd be in your way. You don't want girls along,
I mean what would happen if there were strikebreakers and
trouble and riots in the streets. Then where would you be, I mean
if we were with you . . .
NORMAN: You could tell us more about Vancouver . . . about
the political situation . . . What I always say is, if you're working
for something, you've got to know what you're working for, I
mean, working with, you've got to know the ins and outs of the
whole situation, what I mean is, maybe we could talk.

> *During MARJORIE's speech, at "It's time for
> action . . .", the set-up for the Hudson Bay Riot
> begins. It is done very noisily by RCMP officers.*

MARJORIE: My father says the time for talk is past. It's time for
action and he and my mother and I are all going to the big rally in
Stanley Park and my mother's lodge is going to form a big heart
on the hill and the heart is going to be all mothers . . .
DOC SAVAGE: Okay, fellows, there's a riot at the Hudson Bay
Store. Everybody get back to their divisions!
MARJORIE: And they're going to hold a banner and the banner
will say "Mothers Support the Relief Camp Marchers." I think
that's beautiful and I'm going to help paint the banner.

The Hudson Bay Riot includes confrontations between strikers and police, a lot of noise and confusion and the striker's snake dance — they move quickly, arms linked together, weaving back and forth to avoid making a target for police.

GARTH breaks out of the "snake" and the riot freezes.

GARTH: We were now marching past the Hudson Bay Store. Someone cries out "There's no guards at the Bay," so the whole column of men just turned left and into the store.

This is Division Number 3 and they're a bunch of smart talkers. One of the young fellows is standing on a chair, making a speech and all the girls are gawking at him. A girl screams. There's a whole regiment of police barring the doors to the store and we're inside with them. Fearful. They all line up against one wall. I'm standing, looking down the aisle between the glove counter and the stationery. There's a battalion of police down there with billies.

Our boys, they're youngsters for the most part, are standing there like boulders. The police haven't even started moving yet.

GARTH runs back into the snake which manoeuvres for a five count or so before he breaks out again.

GARTH: They start to move.

Well, I waded right in, of course.

Yes sir, I've always thought fast on my feet. Cowboy Jack Monaghan and I were always regular hellers for brawling.

Two of them come at me. They're both big. I go for the biggest one, put him out of action while I've got the advantage of surprise.

One. Two. He's down. I ploughed him. A powerhouse.

His friend has got me behind. I run at the counter with him still holding on. I throw him over my shoulder. Do that with a twist in the shoulder muscles, here, used to call that the Winnipeg piledriver in my fighting days. He comes up at me again and I rassle him down. *(Snake)* One of the big fellows picked me up then, threw me right through the air at the wall.

Now that made me mad. When I get mad, the fighting gets serious.

There was glass breaking. I was standing there and one of the boys runs at the bulls. Bounced right off and into a display case. He

40

came out of it with the glass still crashing, cuts all over him and blood running into his eyes.

Snake. Which continues until a shot is fired.

McGEER: His Majesty the King charges and commands all persons assembled here immediately to disperse and peacefully to depart to their habitations or to their lawful business upon the pain of being found guilty of an offense for which, upon conviction, they may be sentenced to imprisonment for life.

God save the King.

I'm the mayor of Vancouver, Gerry McGeer. I've been forced to read the Riot Act because of extensive property damage in the streets, here in Victory Square and especially in the Hudson Bay Store.

> *As the strikers trail off in one direction, a spotlight comes up on PETE LOWE.*

PETE: We walk around the streets at night to kill time, so we can sleep in late the next day. By doing so, we exist on two meals a day.

What do we see while putting in the hours? What do we think about?

We see a great many people going to shows, to this and that. Young couples, who seem to be enjoying themselves, well-dressed and acting as if the world isn't so bad after all. People who have homes and kids and all the rest of it. People who seem to have faith in the future.

We think that something is wrong. We can't do as they do. We must go around lonely and dejected. No home life to enjoy, shut off from all social existence. No laughter in our hours. No hope in our young lives.

We see wonderful things in the stores. Food! Clothes! Books! And shiny cars line the streets. But none such for us. Outside looking in! Or in jail looking out. Are we criminals, unwanted by society? Are we lunatics who are to be shunned? What's wrong with us?

We think of marriage and homes, just like others have. Can't even have a friend or two! Shunned like lepers of early times, we are left to our fate. Slave camps, jail or else the salt chuck.

Because we have the guts to fight for our inherited rights we are put in jail. Called Reds and a lot of other meaningless names.

41

We see . . . we think. We see red . . . and we think Red. Can you blame us? Would you like to have us lie down like a bunch of spineless whelps and be contented as slaves? Is that all our grandfathers toiled for? Canada . . . young nation . . . letting her youth go to hell! We who should be the pride of the nation are the derelicts! The curse!

I leave it to you. Where do we go from here?

> *Where we go is to an area of the stage where all the lights available are banged up as quickly as possible, while any set-up necessary continues. The pace of the next scene is frantic. Strikers are in and out all the time for new cans and tags.*

ED: I'll put this chair here, Red.
EVANS: Thanks, Staple.
DOC SAVAGE: Table coming through. ,
EVANS: Move it right in there. *(When the table, chairs, etc, are set, the telephone rings)*   Hello . . . Yes, Red Evans here. Tell them not to worry about getting arrested . . .   *(DOROTHY and MARJORIE enter chattering)*   Quiet, girls, quiet please, I'm on the telephone. Yes, if one of them gets arrested we'll send two more out in his place. Right. Good-bye.
DOROTHY: Well, Mr. Evans, we're ready for anything.
MARJORIE: I've got ten pencils sharpened.
DOROTHY: And I've got a chart made. It goes up to $4,000.

> *BRIDGES enters. EVANS and the girls applaud. It is a small ceremony for the first striker to return to the tag day office. The telephone rings and EVANS answers it.*

BRIDGES: Say, this is tough. People kept moving me from in front of their stores . . .
MARJORIE: You're the first!
BRIDGES: Move on. Down the street, they'd say. You can't sell tags here.
MARJORIE: You're the first!
BRIDGES: Yeah, well some of them paid me to move.

> *NICK enters at a run.*

NICK: Am I the first?
MARJORIE: No.
NICK: Oh.
MARJORIE: But you're the second.

NICK: Oh.

PREACHER: Is this the relief camp worker's tag day office?

REPORTER: I'd like to talk to Mr. Red Evans?

PREACHER: *(To REPORTER)* Mr. Evans. This is fine work you're doing. This is what Christ meant when he said help your neighbour.

DOC SAVAGE: I just can't do this anymore, Red. I've been out for three hours and I only collected two cents.

NORMAN: How are we doing?

DOROTHY: We've got six hundred dollars already.

NICK: *(Exits)* I was the second!

DOROTHY: Hey, second, you forgot your tags!

DOC SAVAGE: I'll just sit down over here.

PREACHER: *(To REPORTER)* I'm from the Holy Pentecostal Tabernacle. Have you been born again?

REPORTER: I'm from the *Vancouver Sun*.

EVANS: The *Vancouver Sun*. Who said that?

PREACHER: *(To EVANS)* I'd like to offer up a small prayer for the success of this tag day . . . Oh, Lord, our Heavenly Father . . .

> *EVANS and the REPORTER make their escape as the prayer continues.*

REPORTER: How is the tag day progressing, Mr. Evans?

PETE: *(Enthusiastic)* How are we doing?

DOROTHY: We've got eight hundred dollars already.

> *The telephone rings. DOC answers it.*

DOC SAVAGE: Sorry, wrong number.

BRIDGES: How are we doing?

DOROTHY: We've got $1,000 already.

MARJORIE: *(Very excited)* One thousand dollars! One thousand dollars!

> *She kisses PETE LOWE in her excitement. The PREACHER approaches DOC SAVAGE who is peeling a banana.*

PREACHER: I noticed your head was bowed my son. Have you been born again?

REPORTER: How about a picture, Mr. Evans?

> *EVANS poses against the table but just as the REPORTER lines up his shot the telephone rings and EVANS turns to answer it.*

43

EVANS: Two men arrested in Burnaby? Two men arrested in Burnaby? Two men arrested in Burnaby? *(NORMAN has entered. To NORMAN)* Get three guys downstairs and get out to Burnaby right now.
NORMAN: Right away, Red.
PREACHER: *(To NORMAN as he leaves)* I'm from the Holy Pentecostal Tabernacle. We'd like to see all of you boys down there on Sunday.
REPORTER: The picture, Mr. Evans?
DOC SAVAGE: *(Blocking the shot)* It was awful out there, Red. Three hours. Two cents. I'm not cut out for this kind of work.
EVANS: *(To DOC)* Why don't you make yourself useful. *(The telephone rings)* Why don't you answer the telephone?
DOC SAVAGE: *(To telephone)* Hello. That's right. Steak and eggs to go.

DOC drops the banana peel.

REPORTER: I'm ready for the picture now.

EVANS steps toward the photographer and slips on the banana peel. Consternation.

EVANS: Who put that banana peel on the floor?
DOC SAVAGE: It came in through the window. Someone is throwing banana peels in through the window.
DOROTHY: I guess we have enemies.
PETE: *(Who enters with a banana)* Hey, someone just brought in four whole stalks of bananas. Says they're a donation from the Safeway Store.
EVANS: Don't touch them!
BEAUMONT: Police Constable R.D. Beaumont. What's going on here, some kind of tag day?
DOROTHY: We've got $1,200 already.

There is a small celebration. MARJORIE hugs anyone handy.

BEAUMONT: Have to have a permit for that kind of thing.
EVANS: Tag day. Tag day? No, this is a donation from the Sunday School of the . . . of the . . .
PREACHER: Holy Pentecostal Tabernacle. My name is Reverend Paterson. Have you been born again?
BEAUMONT: *(To PREACHER)* It's Saturday.
PREACHER: Getting to heaven is a week-long job.
DOC SAVAGE: Care to buy a tag, officer?

BEAUMONT: Ah, hah. Who's in charge here?
DOC SAVAGE: *(Pointing)* Red Evans.
EVANS: *(Pointing past BEAUMONT to the door)* That's Red Evans there. 1914 hero. 1935 bum.

> *BEAUMONT turns to investigate as NICK re-enters the office.*

NICK: I was the second guy in Vancouver to get his can filled.
PETE: *(Entering)* Say will someone get those bananas out of the hallway? They're blocking the stairs.
EVANS: Don't touch them.

> *PETE exits.*

BEAUMONT: I'll get to the bottom of this.
DOC SAVAGE: Officer, I think you should know, there are certain subversive elements out to stop us. Someone is throwing banana peels through the window.
DELIVERY BOY: I got two eggs for delivery here.
DOC SAVAGE: Steak and eggs!
DELIVERY BOY: And the manager of the Safeway Store would like to know if you've seen two guys in funny caps run by here with stolen stalks of bananas.

> *BEAUMONT is holding a banana peel as evidence of subversives. He waves it at the DELIVERY BOY who follows him out.*

BEAUMONT: All right. I'm leaving now, but I'm coming back here with a warrant.
REPORTER: *(To EVANS)* The picture, Mr. Evans.
DOC SAVAGE: These aren't even fried eggs.
EVANS: *(He has sat on one)* Who put those eggs on this table?
DOC SAVAGE: Must be those subversives, Red. Infiltrators. And I'm going to find them.
EVANS: Well, go and find them.
DOC SAVAGE: Right. No, I'll wait here till they come to me.
NICK: *(Enters)* I was the second guy in here and here I am back again.
PETE: *(To DOC)* Say, what are you doing here?
DOC SAVAGE: Shut up! I'm busy.
NICK: *(Effectively blocking the REPORTER's last try at a candid shot)* I was the second guy in Vancouver to get his can filled.
REPORTER: That was the last of my film, Mr. Evans.

PETE: Last time I saw him, he was drinking beer in the Hotel Fitzroy.
PREACHER: What?
REPORTER: What?
EVANS: Roy has fits. Hold his head, Marjorie, there's a good girl.
BEAUMONT: All right. I've got a picture of Red Evans here and I've got a warrant for his arrest.
EVANS: Let me see that. Yes, that's Red Evans all right. *(To REPORTER)* Here's your picture, my friend, on your way.
REPORTER: Gee, thanks a lot, Mr. . . . .
EVANS: *(Sings)* Hold the fort for we are coming.
PREACHER: That's a fine old gospel tune, Mr. Evans.
BEAUMONT: *(To EVANS)* You're Red Evans.
DOC SAVAGE: That's right.
EVANS: That's right. *(Meaning DOC)* He's Red Evans.
BEAUMONT: I'll get to the bottom of this.
DOC SAVAGE: When are we going to Ottawa, Red?
EVANS: *(Describing actor playing DOC)* You've got his description, haven't you? He's tall, skinny, dark curly hair.
DOROTHY: We've got more than $4,000, Mr. Evans. We've gone off the chart.

There is a large celebration, cheering, hugging.
BEAUMONT is carried away but recovers.

BEAUMONT: *(To DOC)* Why do they call you Red?
DOC SAVAGE: You must be one of those subversives.
BEAUMONT: You're a dangerous Communist agitator.
DOC SAVAGE: What's that banana doing in your holster?

DOC makes his escape for as much of a chase as is
practical. The PREACHER follows.

PREACHER: That boy is having a fit.
BEAUMONT: You come back here.
DOC SAVAGE: Let me go.
PREACHER: Out, Satan, out.
DOC SAVAGE: When you realize the mistake you're making, you're going to have egg all over your face.
DOROTHY: We've got more than $5,000.
EVANS: $5,000. All that money. It's Saturday. The banks are closed.
DOROTHY: I called the police station. They're sending a guard over.

The telephone rings.

46

EVANS: Yes, that's right chief, we have $5,000. Just a minute.
(To BEAUMONT) It's for you.
BEAUMONT: *(To telephone)* I got him, Chief. I got the
dangerous Communist agitator.
DOC SAVAGE: *(To PREACHER)* Let me go.
BEAUMONT: *(To PREACHER)* Excuse me, sir. That man's a
dangerous Communist agitator.
PREACHER: Out, Satan, out.
BEAUMONT: *(To telephone)* Yes, Chief. Yes, Chief. Yes Chief.
Yes, Chief. Yes, Chief. *(He hangs up)* The Chief says we're going
to store your money in the station over the weekend.
EVANS: Moscow gold.
BEAUMONT: All right. We're all going down to the station.
NICK: *(Racing on)* I was the second banana in the can to get his
Vancouver filled.

> *Blackout. In the back, cowboy whoops. During the
> ANNOUNCER's speech, the contest between calf and
> cowboy is enacted in slow motion.*

ANNOUNCER: Good afternoon ladies and gentlemen, and
welcome to the first event of the afternoon at the Calgary
Stampede. This is the calf-roping contest and our first contestant
today is Mr. Merle Piston. Merle hails from Fir Siding, Alberta, and
I know all his home town folks are going to give this cowboy a big
hand. Merle's in the chute. There's the horn. The calf is out of
the chute. That's a fast little dogie and Merle might have some
trouble there. He's got his rope up. It's a good throw and the calf
is down, that little dogie is down. Merle's dismounting now,
seems to have his foot caught in the stirrup — that'll slow his time
a little. No, he's all right, he's over at the calf. That's one leg. Two.
That's three. That's a pretty good time for Merle. We're waiting
for the official clock on it, but let's have a big hand for Merle,
folks.

> *Fade on large applause from the rest of the cast in the
> audience and MERLE waving his hat around in
> triumph. In this new black, the sound of a gavel on a
> table. Lights come up on a striker's meeting as DOC
> SAVAGE calls for order.*

DOC SAVAGE: All right, fellow workers, we will now hear from
Fellow Worker Neilson with the Treasurer's Report.
NEILSON: The treasury stands at $211.82. That represents an
expenditure, since yesterday, of $150.00 for room vouchers for
1,000 men and two meal vouchers for 1,000 men at 15 cents each.
$3.58 for shoe repair.

There has been a rumbling of voices in the back.

WORKER: Who the hell gets their shoes repaired?
NEILSON: . . . and $6.00 worth of streetcar tickets. This expenditure is balanced by donations received: $68.00 from Canadian Daughters Lodge 347 Bake Sale and Box Social. $300.00 from the Lumberman's Union.

> *The Sergeant at Arms, COSGROVE, is attempting to raise cheers, out of the general rumble of dissatisfaction.*

COSGROVE: Let's hear it for the Lumbermen. Yeahhh.
NEILSON: $15.00 from the Young Communist League. $1.50 Anonymous donation . . . $22.13 Wesleyan Methodist Church . . .
EVANS: Move to accept the Treasurer's Report as read. Do I have a second?
WORKER: Second.
DOC SAVAGE: All in favour?

> *Aye's very weak. General conversation from the cast in the audience.*

DOC SAVAGE: Opposed? Carried. We'll hear from Comrade Staple of the Recreation Committee.
ED: We've got 34 tickets to *Beggars in Ermine*, fellows. That's on at the Orpheum on Granville Street, it has Lionel Atwill in it . . . it's about "a man who loses his legs in a railway accident, loses his wife and child in an influenza epidemic, loses his money in the Wall Street Crash and still manages to come back." We're all going to meet for the two o'clock show tomorrow afternoon. These tickets were kindly donated by Colonel R. H. Armitage.
EVANS: Move a vote of thanks to Colonel Armitage.
DOC SAVAGE: Do we have a second?

> *No second from the floor.*

COSGROVE: I'll second it.

> *From the audience, the following audible dialogue.*

NICK: I hear they got work in the Okanagan.
NORMAN: How you going to get to the Okanagan? One step into the railway yards and the picket committe's going to bust your head in.
COSGROVE: *(Trying to quiet the house)* Nice talk. Nice talk there.

DOC SAVAGE: We'll hear from Fellow Worker Bridges of the
Billeting Committee.
BRIDGES: Fellow Workers, we have a complaint from the
Ukranian Labour Temple, where some of you guys are staying,
about smoking in bed. Some of you boys have been smoking in
bed, and some of the blankets have got holes burned in them.
There is also the possibility of a more serious fire.

In the audience the following dialogue.

NORMAN: What did he say?
PETE: I can't hear him, I got a cigarette in my ear.
COSGROVE: Quiet down, guys.
BRIDGES: I'd like to move that smoking in bed be prohibited.
DOC SAVAGE: All in favour?
NORMAN: I've been smoking in bed since I was twelve years old.
EVANS: We've got discussion on this point.
DOC SAVAGE: Speak to the motion, please.
PETE: I don't give a damn about the motion. I'm smoking in bed
if I feel like it.
DOC SAVAGE: *(COSGROVE, EVANS, BRIDGES and DOC
SAVAGE vote "Aye")* Opposed? *(Everyone else votes "No")*
Carried. We will hear from the Picket Committee.
PETE: The hell with it.
COSGROVE: Thank you, Fellow Worker Chairman Savage.
Fellow Workers, the boys on strike duty in the Longshoreman's
Union have given me a message for you. They want a little
company tomorrow. I'd say they were anticipating trouble with the
bulls but I wouldn't want the police here with us today to think
we weren't going to give them all a warm welcome . . .
BRIDGES: *(In the audience)* I don't know. All I know is I'm
tired of marching around Vancouver.
DOC SAVAGE: That comrade at the back is out of order.
COSGROVE: I'm putting out a call for volunteers.
O'NEILL: Marching around Vancouver, going to goddamn revival
meetings. We want work and wages . . .
COSGROVE: Volunteers for picket duty with the Longshoremen.
Here's a volunteer.

*But it isn't. It is NICK who wants to make a speech
about his growing disillusionment.*

NICK: I don't know how the rest of you feel. I know I'm fed up.
We've had tag days. We've been marching around the city, singing.
We've all talked to everybody we could find. We took over the
museum, we took over the department stores. Somebody's talking

49

about taking over the North Van ferry and sailing back and forth all day. That's as far as we've got and it looks like it's as far as we're going to get.

> *From the audience: "Damn right," "We're all fed up!" etc.*

DOC SAVAGE: You are out of order, Fellow Worker.
NICK: Fellow Worker Chairman, I don't give a good god damn.
DOC SAVAGE: The Sergeant at Arms will take Fellow Worker Sawchuck back to his section.
NICK: Nobody strong arms me. I came down here to talk about . . .

> *Very loud support from the floor, as COSGROVE moves in on NICK. "Leave him alone," etc. EVANS takes over.*

EVANS: Let him talk. *(Nothing happens. Everyone looks at EVANS)* Go ahead, Nick.
NICK: Well, I've been with you since we walked out of Mara Lake Camp. You were talking about work and wages. Sure, I want work and wages and I don't mind asking for them. I do mind being sold down the river by another bunch of talkers. If that's what's happening.
NORMAN: *(Coming up to the platform)* Damn right.
EVANS: Fellow Worker Sawchuck here has a point.
NORMAN: Damn right.

> *EVANS whips the meeting to a new frenzy in the next section and wins them back to the cause.*

EVANS: We've been here in Vancouver for two months. We've talked to Jeremiah Jesus McGeer, we've talked to the Premier of British Columbia. They know we're here, boys. They don't care. They tell us we're the responsibility of the Dominion Government. They want to play political football. Many of us are thinking we could spend the rest of our lives marching up and down Granville Street. Not the Promised Land, is it?
NORMAN: Came down here to get some action.
EVANS: What do you think we should do about it?
NORMAN: Nick's telling you. You're not doing anything but marching us around. That's bugger all.
EVANS: This is a democratic association. This is the Relief Camp Worker's Union. We work together . . . We need your help . . .
NORMAN: We've been helping you for two months.

50

ED: You can count me out of it.
EVANS: Solidarity . . .
ED: Stuff your solidarity up your ass.
EVANS: How are we going to get work and wages?
NORMAN: That's for you to tell us.
ED: Another bright idea like coming to Vancouver.
EVANS: There's a suggestion from the floor.
EVANS: Fellow Worker Peter Lowe has a suggestion. Get him, Cosgrove.
ED: Where is he?
O'NEILL: Who's Peter Lowe?

COSGROVE leads PETER LOWE to the front of the audience. He looks to EVANS for his cue.

PETE: Well, I say, on to Ottawa.
DOC SAVAGE: State your proposal as a motion, Peter Lowe.
EVANS: Moved that the Relief Camp Workers proceed to Ottawa by C.N.R. and C.P.R. freight to put their proposals before the Prime Minister of Canada.
PETE: R.B. Bennett!
COSGROVE: On to Ottawa!

Over general shouts of "On to Ottawa!," "Sure, now we're talking," etc., a WOMAN enters with a guitar. She takes over the striker's meeting area. They do not notice her. They proceed during her song to construct the train and mount it. The song is straightforward.

WOMAN:
He was just a boy chasing gophers
Teasing the dogs and the mule
He used to ride our old plough horse
Before his first day of school

Where is my boy tonight
Oh, where is my boy tonight
I miss him so 'cause I love him you know
Where is my boy tonight

Filled with the lust of a rover
Sunshiney weather or rain
Happy-go-lucky he rambles
Riding the rods of a train

51

No destination concerns him
His transient companions unknown
Some mother's boy is a wanderer
Off in the wide world alone.

> *A train bell and a loud cheer as the train leaves Vancouver. Everyone is waving goodbye. The train picks up speed. Train noise continues softly under each "mind-trace."*

NORMAN: A thousand guys. All hanging on to one train and all with one idea. On to Ottawa!

ED: See the people back along the siding getting smaller and smaller. And you turn around and there's the mountains, right in front of you. We'll be in Ottawa before we know it.

O'NEILL: 10:10 Seaboard Freight. It's like riding a pony through the Cypress Hills. It's like watching a storm come up.

PETE: I am so excited. I am so excited. I am so excited.

GARTH: I've been to Rio de Janiero. I've been through the Panama Canal. But I never been to Ottawa.

DOC SAVAGE: When I get to Ottawa, I'm going to ask R. B. Bennett for a cup of coffee and a good used car.

NICK: If I can just get over to the side of this boxcar before we pass this river. We must be going fifty-five miles an hour. We'll be in Ottawa before tomorrow.

BRIDGES: When R. B. Bennett sees us marching down the street in Ottawa, he won't know what to do. He'll crap his drawers. He'll have to give us work and wages. Fifty cents an hour. We'll be millionaires!

> *Everyone cheers and the lights go black.*

Act Two

*In the blackout, the sound of the train, which slows
to a halt as the lights come up full. The strikers are
cold, tired, hungry, sleeping in shifts and holding each
other onto the top of the boxcar. COSGROVE is the
first man off the train.*

PETE: Where are we?
COSGROVE: Kamloops.
PETE: Where are the girls of Kamloops?
ED: Where is everybody?
COSGROVE: You guys stay on the train till I give you the signal.
(A bell rings) Okay, boys, get down now. I'll be back in a minute.
DOC SAVAGE: Sawchuck, you're sitting on my foot.
NICK: Yeah, well it kept you on the train all night, didn't it?
PETE: I'm cold.
DOC SAVAGE: Nope, you're feverish, kid. You better stay here
while we go into town. Maybe we'll bring you back some of that
good Kamloops grub.
GARTH: Feed a cold and starve a fever.
ED: Are they going to feed us?
NORMAN: They have to feed us.
COSGROVE: Good news, fellows. We're all going down to the
Orange Lodge. They got something for us down there.
O'NEILL: My foot's asleep. Both my feet.
COSGROVE: Okay, somebody help Paddy down. He jumps off
and he's going to break both his legs. Okay, boys, form up.
Forward march.
DOC SAVAGE: We don't have to march, Cosgrove. There's
nobody watching.
PETE: Where are they?
NORMAN: Let's wake them up a little.
ED:
Hold the fort for we are coming
Union men be strong
Side by side we battle . . .

*At "Battle" there is a jagged effect, rather like a bad
jump cut in a film. The men are berating an imaginary
janitor at the Orange Lodge.*

NORMAN: What do you mean there's no food?
O'NEILL: There's supposed to be food here.
COSGROVE: Look, my information says . . .
NORMAN: Come on, Nick . . .
NICK: Norman?
NORMAN: We can do better on our own. Come on.
NICK: We can't, Norman . . .
ED: We've been on that train ten hours.
DOC SAVAGE: Oh, shit.
PETE: Well, I'm not moving till they feed me. Come on, you guys.
COSGROVE: Sure.
BRIDGES: I can't move.
PETE: Sure. If we stay here, they'll have to feed us.

> *They all sit down, huddling close to each other and miserable. After a moment of very miserable silence, PETE starts to giggle.*

ED: What are you laughing at?
NORMAN: Somebody shut that guy up.

> *PETE falls over NORMAN, still giggling and NORMAN starts giggling in spite of himself.*

PETE: I can hear my stomach growling.
DOC SAVAGE: *(Laughing)* Oh, Jesus.
PETE: It's saying "steak and onions."
NORMAN: Apple pie and ice cream.

> *All the boys begin to laugh, they are listening to each other's stomachs, hearing all about their favourite foods.*

DOC SAVAGE: Steak and onions. Steak and eggs.
O'NEILL: R. B. Bennett with an apple in his mouth.

> *They ad lib, the laughter building to a peak and the boys rolling around the floor like bears. EVANS enters. He is too preoccupied to notice.*

EVANS: All right, boys, I've got two more divisions to talk to, so I want to make this short.
PETE: Where's the food, Red?
EVANS: *(Finally realizing the tone of the group, he tries a bad joke, which fails)* Well, there isn't any.
ED: We've been ten hours on that train.

PETE: What do you mean?

DOC SAVAGE: You said there'd be food.

EVANS: Look, I've got twenty-four C.C.F. ladies at work right now. They're going to make up a thousand sandwiches as fast as they can.

O'NEILL: *(Petulant)* What kind of sandwiches?

PETE: That's not even one sandwich each, Red.

EVANS: I'm sorry, boys, something went wrong, it's the best we can do.

COSGROVE: Look Red, I can't tell these boys one thing and lead them all over town and another thing happens. You can't run a division that way. You told me there was going to be food here.

EVANS: I'm sorry, John. The wires crossed, that's all.

NORMAN: Come on, Nick. Let's go.

EVANS: Wait a minute.

NORMAN: I'm not going to starve to death for you.

EVANS: Who's starving?

NORMAN: I'm not going to make it to Ottawa with one sandwich in my belly and neither is anybody else.

NICK: Easy, Norm . . .

EVANS: You're a little hungry, Norm. You're not starving.

NORMAN: We can do better on our own.

EVANS: And when you get to Ottawa? R. B. Bennett's going to meet your train, I guess.

NORMAN: We're not going to get to Ottawa on one sandwich a day.

EVANS: We're going to do better for you. I promise you that.

NORMAN: You already promised . . .

EVANS: But when we get to Ottawa, who is it going to be able to talk from the gut? R. B. Bennett. Iron Heel Bennett with an apple in his mouth? Or guys who've been hungry? I thought you were hungry to get to Ottawa.

NORMAN: Yeah, sure. Sure I am.

EVANS: Okay. Things will be better at the next stop. I promise you.

BRIDGES: What's the next stop?

EVANS: Golden.

EVANS exits. MRS. MOUNTJOY walks into the scene, with her chair and her knitting. The Golden Men's Choir sing, infinitely harmonically, and except where indicated, all of this next section is sung.

CHORUS:
Golden. Golden. Golden, B.C.

MOUNTJOY:
Knit one, purl one
Slip the knit stitch over
Knit one, purl two
Finish off the shoulder
Coal and oil prices may soar
We may well have need of more
But we will weather any weather
In our very woolly sweaters
Knit one, purl one
Slip the knit stitch over
Knit one, purl two
Finish off the shoulder.

There is a knock at the door.

TELEGRAPH BOY. *(Spoken)* I have a telegram for Mrs.
Mountjoy.
MRS. MOUNTJOY. *(Sings)* Yes?
TELEGRAPH BOY. *(Spoken)* May I sing it to you? *(She nods.
He sings)*
This singing telegram which is signed Red
Tells you 2,000 men have to be fed
The road to Ottawa is hard and long
We'll be in Golden at dawn.
MRS. MOUNTJOY: *(Sings)*
Thank you.
Red Evans always loved a joke
Back in our old school-days
But now I fear he's very serious
And means no delays.
What to do? Two thousand men.
A problem very real.
I have it.
The women of the W.A. very well may save the day
Mr. Merriweather's wife might provide a clue
For he wields a butcher knife which might make up
A stew!
A stew! A stew! Might provide the clue!
A stew! A stew! *(She picks up her telephone)* Ring!
Might provide the clue! Ring!
MRS. MERRIWEATHER: *(Answers her telephone. Sings)* Hello?
MRS. MOUNTJOY:
Hello, dear. I have news for you.
I just received a telegram
MRS. MERRIWEATHER: A telegram? Who died?

MRS. MOUNTJOY:
And 2,000 men from the relief camps
Will arrive in Golden tomorrow.
MRS. MERRIWEATHER: 2,000 men?
MRS. MOUNTJOY: We'll have to feed them.
MRS. MERRIWEATHER. What's that again?
MRS. MOUNTJOY: We'll have to greet them warmly.
MRS. MERRIWEATHER: I can't believe this news I hear.

> *There is a knock at the door. It is the WANDERING*
> *COOK who is clearing his throat.*

MRS. MOUNTJOY: It's true, I fear. One moment, dear.
COOK:
I am a cook. I am a cook. I am a cook.
(He steps downstage for his aria)
I am a wandering cook and for work I look
So if you've got cooking that must be done
Look to me for I'm the one.
(Figaro's aria from "Barber of Seville")
Make spaghetti, macaroni, rigatoni and spumoni, ravioli,
cacciatore, pasta fasul.
Pasta fasul, pasta fasul, pasta fasul, pasta fasul!
MRS. MOUNTJOY: *(With the telephone)*
Listen to this, my dear.
COOK:
Make spaghetti, macaroni, rigatoni and spumoni, ravioli,
cacciatore, pasta fasul!
MRS. MOUNTJOY:
What do you think of that, my dear!
Oh! She hung up.
COOK: She hung up?
MRS. MOUNTJOY: Tell me good cook, could you make for us a
beef . . .
COOK: Stroganoff?
MRS. MOUNTJOY: Stew?
COOK: Stew? Ahrrgh! Chi a la donna e mobile!
(MRS. MOUNTJOY runs in fright)
My spaghetti. My macaroni. Mamma mia.
What can I do?
With all my dishes, so delicious
This crazy lady, all she wants is stew!
MRS. MOUNTJOY:
People of Golden, arise! Open your doors!
Open your windows!
MRS. MERRIWEATHER: Open your hearts!

MRS. MOUNTJOY: Two thousand men from the British Columbia Relief Camps are on their way to our fair village.
MRS. MERRIWEATHER: It's true. It's true.
REPORTER:
Just a conservative moment!
I have just heard an ugly rumour
Rearing its ugly head
Our little town of Golden is about to be invaded
By a raggle taggle mob of malcontents.
TOWNSPEOPLE: Malcontents? Malcontents?
REPORTER: Yes, Malcontents.
FAVOURITE SON: You couldn't mean the workers?
REPORTER:
Ha! You call them workers?
What is their leader's name?
ALL: *(Barber shop harmony)*   Red Evans!
REPORTER:
Aha! Bolsheviks! Communists.
Bolshevik Communist dupes!
They'll rend and tear, destroy our town.
You poor people don't know what you're doing.
They'll leave our little town a smoking ruin.
MRS. MOUNTJOY:
Nonsense!
I have known Red Evans since he was a boy.
I know him to be a righteous man . . .
STRIKERS: *(Approaching to the tune of the "Anvil Chorus")*
Hold the fort for we are coming
Union men be strong
Side by side we battle onward
Victory will come.
ALL: *(Barber shop)*   Welcome! Welcome! Welcome!
STRIKERS: *(Same tune)*
We are tired, we are hungry
Won't you help us, please?
TOWN: *(Same barber shop harmonics)*
Welcome! Welcome! Welcome!
MAYOR:
Welcomèd be! Welcomèd be! Welcomèd be!
As Mayor of the village of Golden
I greet you with open arms
With infinite love and compassion
And virtues old fashion . . . èd.
We have preparèd food for you.
STRIKER 1:   Food?
STRIKER 2:   Food?

TOWN: *(Barber shop)* Yes, food!
MAYOR: *(As they exit)* Members of the Ladies Aid have laid the table in the sylvan glade.
REPORTER: *(The last to leave)*
I fear it is too late for Golden
But one battle does not make a war
I think I will hie me away to Ottawa
To inform the Prime Minister
Mr. R. B. Bennett.
That we got big trouble.

> *Exits. All lights bang up in the sylvan glade where the townspeople are laughing.*

TOWN: Ha ha ha ha ha ha ha ha!
MRS. MOUNTJOY: Won't you have some beef stew with cabbage, beets and celery too?
MAYOR:
We have salads for you.
Macaroni salad, Russian salad
Jelly salad and toss-èd salad.
TOWNSMAN: You must have some cauliflower, radishes and rhubarb.
SON: And something I've prepared especially for you to wash it down. Some buttermilk!
COOK: And won't you try our fresh home made bread with creamery butter.
MRS. MERRIWEATHER. Chocolate cake and strawberry shortcake, home made ice cream, apple pie . . .
SON: *(Beginning a chorus which everyone joins)*
They're eating! They're eating. They're really, really eating.
They're eating! They're eating! They're really, really eating!
STRIKER 1:
Golden days in Golden
Open hearts of Gold.
STRIKER 2:
This is hospitality
That keeps away the cold.
STRIKER 1:
We love it here, we love you
Love your cabbage, love your stew.
STRIKER 2:
Oh, never end this golden day
We wish that we could stay.

But in the distance, there are heard the first few notes of "Hold the Fort." All action stops. They are repeated.

STRIKERS: *(To the tune of the "Anvil Chorus")*
That's Red Evans, he's our leader
He recalls our duty
On to Ottawa because
We search for truth and beauty.
Thank you very much for all you've done
We feel much stronger
Now our cause is calling and we cannot stay
here longer.

> *"Hold the Fort" is played as a polka as the STRIKERS dance onto the train. The favourite son says good-bye to his parents, etc. The lights come up on a Cabinet Meeting in Ottawa.*

BENNETT: The Minister of Trade and Commerce, Mr. Harry Stevens, has resigned from the Cabinet.

I have accepted his resignation.

Certain findings of the Royal Commission on Price Spreads, which Mr. Stevens chaired, twisted out of context and unfortunately sensationalized by the gutter press, have caused a great deal of embarrassment to good friends, good Canadians, loyal supporters of this party. I refer in particular to Sir James Flavelle of Simpsons Department Store.

Certain statements in Mr. Stevens preliminary findings could give the impression that Simpsons Department Store exploited labour in the garment trade. Mr. Stevens would have the country believe that Simpsons Department Store is a sweatshop.

I try to understand what kind of a man could betray his leader and his party in such a manner. That man has done me irreparable personal harm.

Judge not lest you be judged, the Scripture has it. I have read six verses of Scripture every day of my life. I do not judge. I try to understand a man's betrayal.

I am a man. I seek and reach out as all men seek and reach out, for understanding. I do not understand betrayal.

I have a man's feelings. I feel pleasure in simple things. I feel great joy in work. I have friends and a man's trust in his friends. I might have thought that Harry Stevens was my friend.

Oh, I have my faults. It might be said that I am impatient, quick to anger. Anger is a fault but it is understandable. Anger is a human reaction to deceit, denial, as Peter forsook his Lord, as Judas sold his Lord for silver, wilful, headstrong, arrogant self-interest. Mutinous, treasonable betrayal!

Lights down in Ottawa and up on the entrance to the spiral tunnel.

DOC SAVAGE: That's the spiral tunnel up ahead. That's the long one, the big fellow.
ED: Well, I'm not afraid a bit.
DOC SAVAGE: Nothing to be afraid of. Unless you're afraid of the dark.

Stage goes to half light.

ED: Yeah, it's kind of dark in here.
DOC SAVAGE: Wait till you can't see the end.
ED: How long does it take?
DOC SAVAGE: Twenty minutes.
ED: Smokey.

Everyone else on the train is choking, coughing, holding their caps up over their faces.

DOC SAVAGE: Put your handkerchief over your face. Usually, just a couple of guys on the train, they get off, climb up and meet the tunnel where it comes out.
ED: We're going to die in here.
DOC SAVAGE: No, we aren't.
ED: I'm getting off.
DOC SAVAGE: No, you aren't.
ED: I can't breathe. I'll meet the train at the top.
DOC SAVAGE: You've got to climb outside. You're inside a fucking mountain, for Christ's sake.

ED screams. He keeps screaming and struggling for the edge of the boxcar. DOC SAVAGE holds him down. DOC SAVAGE's speech will probably not be heard except when ED runs out of breath momentarily.

DOC SAVAGE: Look, Staple, look Ed, don't think about it. Think about something else. I ever tell you when I was being a tour guide on Lake of the Woods? That's a fine life. Running those little boats all around. Nothing out there but you and the water

61

and islands. They probably have forty thousand islands in Lake of the Woods and every one is beautiful.

ED: Let go of me. I'm getting off.

DOC SAVAGE: Get people coming down from Winnipeg, looking like the city worries them and that lake makes them look alive again. Night comes down, you can hear loons calling out across the water. Blueberries. You never tasted blueberries like that, Ed. Look Ed. There's a light up ahead.

> *Blackout on the train and lights up quickly on another area of the stage where the Prophetic Bible Hour Ladies Choir is singing something like "I Like the Christian Life," or, "Turn Your Radio On." During the song, the train is dismantled. BIBLE BILL ABERHARDT is standing by and when the song is over, he speaks.*

ABERHARDT: Thank you, ladies.

Fellow Christians, our bible study tonight is a story that each and every one of us heard first at our mother's knee. I would like to talk to you about the exodus of the Israelites from the land of Egypt and I would like to draw your attention to the similarities between their experiences in the desert and our life today in the Province of Alberta.

There is a famine in the land. And the question that the Israelites asked of Moses and the question that the people of Alberta are asking today is, "What are we going to do about our famine in our land?"

The Israelites went to the land of the Canaanites and the Hittites and the Amorites . . .

WORKER: Work and wages!

ERHARDT: And the Perrizites. And the Hivites and the Jesusites which was the land of milk and honey. With Moses as their leader. Some of the people of Alberta are asking where are our leaders today and I can tell you where your leaders are today. Your leaders are among us. Look about you. There are men whose religion is still intact. There are honest men among you.

Fellow Christians, you have a responsibility and it is your responsibility to exercise that responsibility. Your responsibility is to gather together today for me one hundred honest men.

For when we know the names of one hundred honest men, we will know the names of one hundred honest men. To lead us.

I know you will sit down after this broadcast and talk it over with your family, which man in your community will you choose?

I'd like to offer up a short prayer for guidance in our choice. Oh Lord, our Heavenly Father, please guide us, Amen.

Why do I ask you to send me the names of one hundred honest men? Because only a man who is fundamentally honest will be able to lead us out of the Land of Canaan . . .
WORKER: Work and wages!
ABERHARDT: And into the land of economic democracy.

Do you doubt that this is possible? I suppose that one day many years ago, a man held up a little piece of paper, a stamp, and said that when attached to a letter it would carry that letter all around the world. Many doubted the truth of his statement but he had a vision and that vision has become a reality.

It's just like the circulation of the blood. The blood passes down the arm, through the body and into the leg, through the leg to the foot and back up the leg, down the other leg to the foot, back up to the arm and the head and the brain, down the other arm, back through the heart and the lungs to the foot and everytime the blood passes through the heart and the lungs it receives another $25 per month from the Social Credit Government.

And that is why, ladies and gentlemen, this same blood can pass all the way through the Province of Alberta today and through the rest of Canada tomorrow.

> *The marching begins once more. Most of the cast will be citizens of Calgary, watching the parade, but some sense of mass should be achieved by the remaining strikers.*

WOMAN: Hold it, it's a Kodak . . . Reminds me of Harry marching back home with his regiment from the War. But there's more of them and they're just boys, aren't they . . .
LADY POET: . . . Better than the boys in Calgary. Sometimes I don't think the boys around here are interested in anything more than Massey-Harris tractors. I don't think these boys would be like that. That dark-haired one, he looks very sensitive. I'll bet he's read *Anthony Adverse* . . .
TEACHER: All right, class. I want you to take out your history books and read Chapter III silently. You aren't here to gape out the window. You're here to study and to learn.
WOMAN: They're going down to the stadium. Maybe Harry wouldn't mind if we took the Ford and drove by later in the afternoon . . .

RANCHER: What are these goddamned Communists . . .
WOMAN: Harry's not much for strangers but he is one for western hospitality.
RANCHER: 'Scuse me, ma'am.
LADY POET: And his eyes would mist over and he'd turn away. He'd say "Ma'am I guess you recall the words of the poet . . ."
MACILRAITH: What are these goddamned Bolsheviks doing in Calgary? This is R. B. Bennett country.
WOMAN: So many of them.
LADY POET: "I would not love thee half so much loved I not honour more."
WOMAN: Harry laughs at me but sometimes I wish I'd been a man. I wish I could fly a plane. I wish I were an aviatrix. I wish I were marching.
WOULD-BE STRIKER: On to Ottawa. Work and wages. Vancouver to Ottawa. Edmonton to Ottawa.
TEACHER: I don't care what your father thinks of R. B. Bennett, Elizabeth. We're studying Henry VIII. Who can tell me the names of Henry VIII's six wives?
LADY POET: "It is a far, far better thing that I do now than ever I have done before."
BOY: What are these fellows doing marching down 4th Street, Mr. MacIlraith?
MACILRAITH: Why aren't you in school, boy?
RANCHER: Way I look at it, nobody owed these boys a living. This is a big country. There's lots of work for those that want it and my taxes are not going to go to supporting a bunch of no-good lazy, Bolshevik good-for-nothings, all foreigners anyway, should be shipped back where they came from . . . If one of them came out to my ranch . . .
C.C.F.'ER: Way I look at it these boys have the right idea. The whole country's gone crazy and these boys know it.
TEACHER: That's right. Anne of Cleves . . . Anne . . .
LADY POET: "He was born with a gift for laughter and a sense that the world was mad."
WOMAN: Amelia Earhart, for example . . .
MARCHER: This parade goes on for much longer I'm going to lose my liberal sympathies.
WOULD-BE MARCHER: Go to it, boys!
BOY: Go to it, boys!
C.C.F.'ER: Go to it, boys!
WOMAN: If I were an aviatrix, I'd be up there in my Tiger Moth, flying circles around you. I'd be towing a sign saying "On to Ottawa."
RANCHER: One of them came out to my ranch, guess I'd have to tell them that there wasn't any work.

LADY POET: "Ho, ho, ho, he laughed madly."
RANCHER: My ranch isn't doing so well at that. Maybe they got the right idea.
BOY: Work and wages!
C.C.F.'ER: On to Ottawa!
WOULD-BE MARCHER: Talk to Bennett. Tell him what it's like.
RANCHER: Go to it, boys!
WOMAN: We will go down to the stadium. I'll tell Harry we have to do what we can.
TEACHER: There's one more, class. Anne of Cleves. Anne . . .
LADY POET:
"Cannon to the right of them,
Cannon to the left of them . . ."
TEACHER: I don't know what it was. It was a parade of some kind. You aren't in school to watch parades!

> *Blackout. Lights come up on the arena at the Calgary Stampede.*

ANNOUNCER: Good afternoon, ladies and gentlemen and welcome to Dominion Day at the Calgary Stampede. The first event this afternoon is the Brahma Bull Riding and the bull in the chute is R. B. Bennett. Bennett has proven to be the toughest bull to ride at this meet, so it should be an exciting contest. Bennett has been purchased by an English syndicate and at the end of the meet, will be retired.

Attempting to ride Bennett today is Red Evans. Red hails from Drumheller by way of Vancouver and Toronto and I know we all wish him the best of luck. Red's an old hand with the bulls so we could have some interesting results here this afternoon.

There goes the horn. They're out of the chute. Red is holding on but this Bennett is a lot of bull. He's a tough one, ladies and gentlemen, but Red's a fighter. Oh no, he's through. Bennett's turning back at him, ladies and gentlemen. Get out there, Red. Get moving . . .

> *Lights fade as the rodeo clown, COSGROVE, leads BENNETT away from EVANS. Lights up on another small area of the stage, a park in Regina.*

NORMAN: This is real nice.
ED: The last time I was home, there was a big huge party. Everyone in the district. I danced so long I had to take my shoes off. Then I danced so long after that I wore my socks right through.
NICK: We aren't home yet.

65

NORMAN: Close enough.

NICK: Regina? Doesn't take very much to make you happy.

NORMAN: I think Mr. and Mrs. Dougherty, they remind me of my folks.

NICK: They aren't your folks.

NORMAN: They invited me home for supper. You should have come with me, Nick.

NICK: Sure.

ED: What did you have for supper?

NORMAN: Mr. Dougherty makes wine in his cellar. They're Catholics, but they're real nice people.

NICK: I'm glad you like it here.

NORMAN: After supper, we listened to the radio. Those programmes they have on the radio are quite funny.

ED: What did you have for supper?

NORMAN: And I told them a little bit about the strike. They were very interested.

NICK: Real night on the town.

NORMAN: Well, it must have been getting on for ten o'clock so Mrs. Dougherty made some tea and they all went to bed and I came back here and played poker with Cunningham.

NICK: I'm glad you're so happy here because R. B. Bennett says Regina's as far as we get.

ED: What did you have for supper?

NORMAN: I told you this morning. When we were lining up for sandwiches.

ED: Tell me again.

NICK: Did you hear me?

NORMAN: Sure. I heard that story too, Nick. But he can't do that. We're going to Ottawa. There's two thousand guys . . .

NICK: Any trains with more than four cars are re-routed through Saskatoon.

NORMAN: Come on!

NICK: They say they're going to set up a special camp at Dundurn, an internment camp.

NORMAN: I met a guy from Dundurn, came down to join the trek. There's guys from Edmonton, Calgary, Swift Current have joined us . . .

ED: There's two thousand guys in Winnipeg just waiting till we get there.

NICK: We aren't going to get there.

NORMAN: Sure we are.

GARTH: What we need is military tactics.

NORMAN: Mrs. Dougherty is going to make a quilt.

NICK: You're goofy, Norman.

NORMAN: The quilt will have the relief camp marchers going to Ottawa. Every worker will be carrying something that represents his trade. They'll all be looking off into the distance . . .

ED: Hey, maybe she could embroider "Hold the Fort" all around the edge.

NICK: You're both goofy.

NORMAN: There's too many guys. Not even R. B. Bennett can stop two thousand working people who know what they want and how they're going to get it.

NICK: As long as all they want is home made cookies.

NORMAN: *(To ED)* You want to play some softball?

ED: Sure. Come on, Garth.

NICK: Look, there's going to be trouble.

NORMAN: Oh, sure.

NICK: There are Mounties everywhere. Marching up and down. There are Mounties pretending that they're strikers.

ED: Sure. Me, for example.

NICK: How long were we supposed to be here?

NORMAN: Three days.

ED: Evans has everything organized. He'll tell us when to move.

NICK: How long have we been here?

NORMAN: I don't know.

NICK: Five days!

ED: *(To NORMAN)* Are you a Mountie or a striker?

NORMAN: Oh no, Mr. Mountie, don't shoot. I'm just a poor working boy on the way to see the Prime Minister.

NICK: Right. We said we were going to Ottawa. We can't just stop here because the weather's fine. Look the people here have been good to us, maybe they could get some cars and trucks together, drive us to Winnipeg. We can hop the freights from there.

GARTH: Ranger tactics. Good for work in the field. When we got to meetings, expecting trouble. First of all we go out in the woods and we each catch a skunk.

NICK: That's a great idea.

GARTH: We put all the skunks in gunny sacks and we take them along to the meetings. When the police come in, we let the little creatures out of the sacks.

NICK: He's cock-eyed.

GARTH: I've seen battle.

NICK: Won the Great War single-handed.

ED: War of 1812.

NICK: I could get to Ottawa.

NORMAN: I'm going over to Dougherty's. Come on, Ed. They said maybe I could spend the night.

ED: Dougherty's probably working for the Mounties.

NICK: I could get to Ottawa by myself, if I didn't have to drag you three everywhere. I'd get right into R. B. Bennett's office.
GARTH: Sure.
NICK: And he'd make me General Manager of the Eddy Match Company.
GARTH: You wouldn't want to do that, would you, son?
NICK: What?
GARTH: You wouldn't want to go anywhere if we weren't following behind you.

CONVENOR enters.

CONVENOR: *(To audience)*   Thank you for coming to our picnic which is in honour of the eight man delegation now on their way to Ottawa to talk with our Prime Minister R.B. Bennett. We hope that you'll take this opportunity to get to know some of the young strikers.

> *The STRIKERS should begin circulating through the audience at this point, perhaps passing out song sheets, or food, or just making conversation.*

We hope you all have your song sheets. We hope you remembered to bring your box lunches. I would like to thank Mrs. Amy Gelford for making the ribbons which identify our picnic officials. I would like to thank Mrs. Maisy Gilbert for leading us in that lovely prayer for the success of the Strikers Committee. I would like to thank Mrs. Alice Friedrich for her work with the Box Lunch Committee and of course a special vote of thanks goes to Miss Elizabeth Meadowcroft for her dramatic reading of the inspirational poem "No Port in a Storm." Miss Meadowcroft was once especially singled out by our Governor-General, the Earl of Bessborough at a drama festival in Guelph, Ontario. I have a few announcements. Will the Regina Boys Band please meet at the East Door? Will the contestants for the egg and spoon race please register with Mr. Richards? He is wearing a blue and yellow striped ribbon.

> *The music begins. The Cast will dance "The Butterfly" or maybe a schotisse, after which the house lights should come on. There will be an open polka, cast members inviting the audience. If possible the floor where the audience sits should have some open space so that those who don't want to dance on stage can still dance. In this section, if the budget is available, strikers who don't get dancing partners can continue*

*to hand out food. The polka ends when demand
seems to warrant it. A last waltz clears stragglers off
the stage. While the confrontation is being set up,
COSGROVE sings.*

COSGROVE:
All along the water tank
Waiting for the train
A thousand miles away from home
Sleeping in the rain
I walked up to a railway bull
To give him a line of talk
He said if you have money
I'll see that you don't walk
I haven't got a nickel
Not a penny to my score
Get off, get off, you railroad bum
He slammed the boxcar door.

Yodel-ay-ee. Yodel-ay-ee-o.

They put me off in Moose Jaw
That's a town I dearly love
Wide open spaces all around me
The moon and stars shine up above
I've seen enough of soup lines
I'm tired of union halls
I'm on my way from Montreal
I'm going back to Ocean Falls.

Yodel-ay-ee. Yodel-ay-ee-o.

MR. BENNETT ushers the STRIKERS into his office.

BENNETT: We will get your names first, commencing on the left.
Your name?
EVANS: Arthur H. Evans.
BENNETT: You used to be in Alberta, if I remember right?
EVANS: I have been in various parts.
BENNETT: You were in Drumheller in my time?
EVANS: Yes.
BENNETT: Where is your home?
EVANS: Vancouver, B.C.

COSGROVE enters, late.

BENNETT: And your name?
COSGROVE: John Cosgrove.

BENNETT: Where is your home?

COSGROVE: In British Columbia at the present time.

BENNETT: And the next?

O'NEILL: Stuart O'Neill, Vancouver.

BENNETT: And your name.

SAVAGE: Robert Savage.

BENNETT: Where is your home, Mr. Savage?

SAVAGE: Vancouver.

BENNETT: And your name?

MARTIN: Richard Martin, Vancouver.

BENNETT: And the next?

McAULEY: Mike McAuley, Vancouver.

BENNETT: And the next?

NEILSON: Peter Neilson, Vancouver.

BENNETT: Does that comprise the delegation?

EVANS: Yes, sir.

BENNETT: Well now, who speaks for you?

EVANS: I have been elected as spokesman.

BENNETT: Yes, Mr. Evans, we shall be glad to hear you.

EVANS: We have a set of six points with respect to the relief camps.

In the first place, the relief camp situation in British Columbia presents an absolutely hopeless outlook for the men in these relief camps, for the youth. Some of them in British Columbia have not in three years been inside the four walls of a home.

We find conditions have only been improved through organization. When committees have attempted to function, the members have been blacklisted. What it really amounts to is blacklisted into starvation.

Our organization, the Worker's Unity League . . .

BENNETT: What is the name of the League?

EVANS: The Worker's Unity League, called a conference since blacklisting had increased.

One case is that of McCauley. He was distributing literature in the camps on the Princeton Road, working class literature.

BENNETT: Communist literature?

EVANS: Not necessarily Communist literature.

BENNETT: But it was Communist literature.

EVANS: I say it was the Relief Camp Worker's Journal which is not a Communist journal. He was savagely attacked in the evening by a representative of the Department of National Defence and by the Provincial Police. After two o'clock in the morning he was taken out of bed . . .

BENNETT: In other words, he got into a fight with a policeman.

70

EVANS: In other words, he was dragged out of bed at two o'clock.
BENNETT: Before he went to bed he got into a fight with a policeman!
EVANS: That is not correct.
BENNETT: What is it, then? He got into a fight with the Provincial Police?
EVANS: He did not. He was lying in his bed.

On the basis of grievances like these, a walk out was approved.

Our first demand is for work with wages, a minimum of fifty cents per hour for unskilled labour, union wages for skilled workmen. The present cost of maintenance of the relief camps is $45 per month per man. The cost of this demand would mean $60 a month and the workers would buy their own board and all their clothing.

Our second demand is that all relief projects be covered by the Workmen's Compensation Act.

Our next demand is for recognition of camp committees. The rules of the Department of National Defence regarding complaints say that superintendents and foremen will discuss complaints with individuals. But when this has been attempted, the man has been blacklisted and chased out of camp.

Our next demand is that all relief camps be taken out of the Department of National Defense, with no military regulations. This is one of our central demands.

Our next demand is for a genuine system of social and economic insurance.

Our next demand is that the workers in the camps be guaranteed the democratic right to vote. They have been denied the right to vote on the grounds that they have no habitation and that they are being provided for by the government.
BENNETT: How old are you, Mr. Evans?
EVANS: 46.
BENNETT: How old are you, Mr. Cosgrove.
COSGROVE: 35.
BENNETT: How old are you, Mr. Savage?
SAVAGE: 23.
BENNETT: Where were you born?
SAVAGE: Birkenhead, England.
BENNETT: Where were you born, Mr. Cosgrove?
COSGROVE: Rothesay, Scotland.
BENNETT: Where were you born, Mr. Evans?
EVANS: I was born in Toronto, Ontario.

BENNETT: You were born in Toronto, you say.
EVANS: I am sure of it, and several of my family; my father was born there. We have been in this country something like 112 years.
BENNETT: And how old are you, Mr. O'Neill?
O'NEILL: 36.
BENNETT: Where were you born?
O'NEILL: Newfoundland.
BENNETT: And the next?
MARTIN: I was born in London, England.
BENNETT: How old are you?
MARTIN: 31.
BENNETT: Does anybody else desire to make any observations?
COSGROVE: I am going to speak on the Compensation Act. Being first aid man in the camps, I have seen many accidents take place. In one case, in particular, Case 346 at Yale, B.C. fell 75 feet down a mountain side. He had a gash in his head six inches long and suffered 21 days with slight concussion of the brain. For 12 days he had no doctor. I had to doctor him.
MARTIN: We are ready to talk business on the six demands.
BENNETT: We have listened with much interest to what you men have had to say. With the exception of one of you, who has a record we will not discuss, you were born outside of Canada, and in the country from which you come, I was told the other day there are one million men who have no work and never will have. With respect to single unemployed men who have drifted into the Province of British Columbia, we said we would provide one, food, two, shelter, three, clothing for such unemployed persons.

We have given you good food, good shelter and good clothing.

There was no compulsion and no discipline. The Department of National Defense operated these camps because they had the equipment, tents and they had the personnel.

It was felt that if the men went into camps and did some work or chores they might be better off than receiving merely relief, and that they would get some exercise and keep themselves fit. For that they received the twenty cents as a gratuity paid by the state.

Agitators went into these camps, agitators representing a form of government that we will not tolerate in Canada, agitators representing Communism which we will stamp out in this country with the help of the people of Canada.

The Unity League is not unknown to us. We are fully seized of all the circumstances in connection with the operations of the Unity League. We know from necessity where its agents are. They endeavour by force, if necessary, to destroy the institutions of this country.

72

Leaving Vancouver, you illegally trespassed upon railway property, endangering human life.

You reached Regina. At Regina, your numbers are now camped.

Now you ask for work. At one place it was for relief. At another place it is for work and wages. You have not shown much anxiety to get work, not much anxiety to get work. It is the one thing you do not want. What you want is this adventure in the hope that the organization which you are promoting in Canada may be able to overrun government and break down the forces that represent law and order.

You talk of Workmen's Compensation Act. Every case in which a man has been injured has been investigated by the authorities. The case to which Mr. Cosgrove referred of a man falling is something which may happen to any man anywhere and may more easily happen climbing on a freight train that most places I know.

I do ask you young men, at your age, whether or not you think you are playing the part of good citizens when we are supplying you with the conditions of home, because you are homeless men. Now you suddenly say: We are going to violate laws and march to Ottawa. March to Ottawa for what purpose. What purpose?
EVANS: The purpose is to demand from you this programme of work and wages.

You referred to us as not wanting work. Give us work and see whether we will work. This is an insidious attempt to propagandize in the press on your part. Anybody who professes to be Premier and uses such despicable tactics is not fit to be Premier of a Hottentot village.
BENNETT: I come from Alberta. I remember when you embezzled the funds of your union and were sent to the penitentiary.
EVANS: You're a liar. I was arrested for fraudulently converting these funds to feed the starving. I say you are a liar if you say I embezzled.
BENNETT: I know your record in the penitentiary at New Westminster, your record in the penitentiary elsewhere.
EVANS: I was never in penitentiary at New Westminster. You don't know what you are talking about.
BENNETT: Where was it?
EVANS: I know your . . .
BENNETT: You are here deluding a number of young men.
EVANS: I have stated that I used the funds for hungry people instead of sending them to Indianapolis to a bunch of pot-bellied business agents.

BENNETT: I was referring to the second time you were sent to the penitentiary.
EVANS: Where was the second time? I was never sent a second time to penitentiary.
BENNETT: Jail.
EVANS: Under Section 98 for leading miners in a strike.
O'NEILL: You have accused us of all kinds of things . . .
BENNETT: Nobody has told you the facts and I am trying . . .
O'NEILL: I have ridden in boxcars in France and I sat in a trench and nobody called me a foreigner then.
COSGROVE: I take exception to any personal attack on this delegation and will not . . .
BENNETT: Sit down, Mr. Cosgrove.
COSGROVE: I will not.
BENNETT: Then you will be removed.
EVANS: Then the entire delegation will be removed.
COSGROVE: I will when I have said this. I fought in the war as a boy fifteen years old. I have the interests of this country as much at heart as you have.
BENNETT: You cannot take the government by the throat and demand that anything that pleases your sweet will be done . . .
O'NEILL: Two thousand men in Regina . . .
BENNETT: Who put them in that state of mind?
O'NEILL: You did!
EVANS: I propose we do not interject anymore. We will take the rest of what he has to say to the workers and citizens of Canada.
BENNETT: That is your privilege so long as you keep within the law and the minute you step beyond it, Mr. Evans, you will land where you once were.

You were asking for work with wages, and a minimum of 50 cents per hour for unskilled labour. So far as that is possible, it is being carried on from one end of Canada to the other. When you suggest in your first demand that these camps be turned into work and wages, that is an impossible situation so far as the Dominion Government is concerned.

Your second demand. No.

Your third demand. Impossible.
O'NEILL: You could have told us all this by wire.
BENNETT: I am going on with this memorandum.

In your fourth demand, you ask for no military control or training in the relief camps. There never has been. It was never suggested there should be.
EVANS: Military rules are published in every camp.
BENNETT: I am familiar with them.

EVANS: You are not.

O'NEILL: There was military training.

BENNETT: Never under the authority of the Department of National Defense.

O'NEILL: What about Point Grey Camp?

BENNETT: That is not a camp where military discipline is maintained.

O'NEILL: You don't seem to know. They wear a uniform and carry rifles . . . there are boys in Vancouver . . . they are on strike with us now.

BENNETT: They are not doing that under the direction of the government.

NEILSON: I am an old soldier, familiar with all forms of government . . .

BENNETT: The government thanks you. Demand No. 5. No. Demand No. 6. No.

That is all that can be said. I want to warn you once more, if you persist in violating the laws of Canada, you must accept full responsibility for your conduct.

EVANS: And you also.

BENNETT: I am prepared for that.

EVANS: So are we.

BENNETT: In order that there may be no misunderstanding you might make known to all those who are with you, that they will be able to go back to their camps, and that as work develops on highways or on any other public undertakings, they will have the opportunity to work, but that a continuance of illegal trespassing upon the property of the railways involving the interruption of mails, the loss of life, and injury to property will not be tolerated. I have nothing more to say.

Good morning, gentlemen, we have been glad to listen to you.

> *RED EVANS joins SAM EAST at another part of the platform. During EAST's appeal, the Ottawa set is struck. Any representation of police are placed at the theatre's exit door. This change can be as noisy as need be. Members of the cast in police uniforms begin to range through the back of the theatre, talking loudly, discussing tactics for clearing the area. Probably just before EAST's appeal for funds, police drag him and EVANS from the platform.*

EAST: My name is Sam East. I have a pastorate here in Regina. I've seen a lot of the boys from the trek in our church. When the Ottawa delegation came back empty-handed, so to speak, a lot of

75

the local people agreed to drive the boys to the Manitoba border. We thought the March to Ottawa should continue. We arranged a truck cavalcade with the co-operation of the Minister of Highways here in Saskatchewan.

We got a mile and a half out of town.

We were stopped by R.C.M.P., Federal Police, wearing their tin hats, with riding crops and pistols.

I told them we had the permission of the provincial government to move on that highway.

I was arrested.

They say that any aid to the strikers is illegal under Section 98 of the Criminal Code. "Anyone who assists persons who are in unlawful association or assembly, in the way of transportation, use of buildings, food and so on, is guilty of an offense."

The strikers are not in unlawful assembly. I was arrested so Federal Police could take me off that highway.

Unlawful assembly? Sure. Most of the boys are over on the other side of town watching a softball game right now.

I'm glad to see so many Reginans at this rally. We're going to ask you for money to help the strikers. We want to show the R.C.M.P. what we think of Section 98.

>As the police move in, two STRIKERS at the door
>to the theatre begin to shout.

STRIKER 1: You can't do that, he's a preacher.
STRIKER 2: Oh, God.

>There are gunshots, sound of breaking glass, screams.
>All from the back of the theatre if that is possible.
>There should be a definite sound threat at the exit or
>exits. EVANS is tussling with a Mountie or Mounties
>on the stage.

>Slowly, the police move down to the front of the
>theatre. The STRIKERS are calling: "They're
>shooting at us. They're moving in with horses. They
>can't do this," etc. The police at the front of the
>theatre have batons. They strike them rhythmically
>against their palms. The house lights come up.

POLICEMAN: All right, folks, we're going to clear this area.

76

POLICEMAN: We've had a little trouble here.
POLICEMAN: There's nothing more to see.
POLICEMAN: Help us along.
POLICEMAN: You're all going home.

> *POLICEMEN ad lib additional dialogue. At the door of the theatre as the audience files out, the STRIKERS are handcuffed to policemen. They tell their own stories of what happened after the riot. All the charges were dropped at the trial the next year, they went to their homes or back to the camps which were disbanded the next year, they went to Spain, they fought in the Second World War, they were arrested for vagrancy, they bought a gas station, whatever.*

Plains Indians used to hunt buffalo by stampeding them over a cliff. That was called a "buffalo jump."

Chronology of Events

October, 1929	Sudden price slumps on the Toronto and Montreal Stock Exchange, and on the Winnipeg Grain Exchange, heralded the arrival in Canada of the Great Depression and the end of the "Roaring Twenties."
July 28, 1930	The Liberal Government of MacKenzie King severely defeated in a federal election by the Conservative Party of R.B. Bennett.
October, 1932	A nationwide system of "Relief Camps" established by the Bennett Government, for single, homeless, and unemployed men.
March 10, 1935	At a Relief Camp Workers' Union meeting in Kamloops, Relief Camp strike planned for April to protest conditions of employment, which at that time consisted of food, housing and payment of 20 cents a day.
April 4, 1935	Beginning of Relief Camp strike.
April 5, 1935	Opening of federally appointed "MacDonald Commission" hearings into Relief Camp conditions.
April 10, 1935	Strikers congregating in Vancouver refused relief by the city.
April 13, 1935	Strikers' Tag Day in Vancouver; over $5000 collected.
April 23, 1935	Riot involving strikers and police at Hudson's Bay Company Store in Vancouver; Mayor Gerry McGeer forced to read the Riot Act.
May 18, 1935	Seizure of Vancouver City Museum by strikers; Relief finally granted by the city.
May 29, 1935	Vote taken to begin a mass trek by freight train to Ottawa.
June 3, 1935	Departure from Vancouver of the On to Ottawa Trek.
June 4, 1935	Arrival of Trek in Kamloops.
June 6, 1935	Arrival of Trek in Golden.

June 8, 1935	Arrival of Trek in Calgary.
June 11, 1935	RCMP Assistant Commissioner in Regina instructed that Trek was to be forcibly stopped in that city.
June 14, 1935	Arrival of Trek in Regina.
June 18, 1935	After negotiations with federal ministers, departure of an eight-man delegation to Ottawa, to present the strikers' six main demands to Prime Minister Bennett.
June 22, 1935	Meeting of delegation to Regina; almost two thousand men camped in Regina; rations exhausted, despite the help of a Citizens' Committee formed to aid the trekkers.
July 1, 1935	Dominion Day rally in Market Square; the Regina Riot.
July 4, 1935	Departure of trekkers from Regina.
October, 1935	After a heavily fought election campaign, the Bennett government defeated in a Liberal landslide victory, returning Mackenzie King to power on a platform that included a commitment to close the Relief Camps.
September, 1936	Last of the Relief Camps closed, by which time many of the participants in the Trek were on their way to fight in the International Brigades in the Spanish Civil War.

GABE

Act One

The action flows freely, without blackouts, between three areas: The Tahiti Room of the Empress Hotel, Jackson's Service Station and an exterior area which is presumably located behind the hotel.

The music for the songs should be improvised to suit the tastes and voices of the company. The effect should be of extemporaneous composition.

The Tahiti Room of the Empress Hotel.

LOUIS and HENRY: *(Sing)*
I got drunk that Friday night
I was pissed north by northeast
There's laws against a one-man war
They should have told me that before
They sent for the police.

I know the Lord loves his soldiers
God loves his soldiers
God loves his soldiers
The Bible tells me so.

I got drunk that Friday night
I got crazy drunk again
Sure I was going to give them hell
Like the crazy bastard Louis Riel
And then the fuzz walked in.

LOUIS: My friends, Gabriel Dumont has pursuaded Louis Riel to come from Montana and live among us for a while. This is a great day for the Metis nation. What he did before Monsieur Riel can do again.
VONNE: Did your friend talk like that in jail, Gabe?
GABE: Better.
VONNE: Best thing I seen in Batoche since the Carling salesman.
LOUIS: *(Showing off)* Louis Riel! Was the maddest, smartest, bravest Metis bastard ever wrote his own treaty. Ever fought for the rights of his people. For their land. Fought for representation.

For his people and for their children. And the white man. The fucking Canadian, listened to him. We didn't listen.

HENRY is distributing goodies, getting in the way.

VONNE: Sit down, Henry.
HENRY: I got beer nuts, and a pepperoni sausage. I got sour cream and onion potato chips. That the kind you like?
VONNE: Shut up, Henry.

LOUIS discovers everyone listening to him. He tails off and dives for his beer bottle.

LOUIS: He was talking about medicare, health insurance, social security . . . Riel was . . . The white government's got all that and the Metis got welfare. Got charity and handouts. You know. For being fool enough . . . Getting . . . thirsty.

VONNE covers for him.

VONNE: Last time you saw Rosie, Gabe, she was running around with a bread bag on a string, trying to fly it like a kite.
GABE: *(Watching LOUIS)* I guess so.
VONNE: Last time you saw me it was in this hotel. It was upstairs. You were treating yourself.
GABE: *(To LOUIS)* Tell them, Louis.
LOUIS: And an Indian agent took some government people into a settlement up north . . . saw all the people living in shacks by the side of a lake . . . went back to Regina and planned a community for them. Sent a construction crew in to build a row of little white cottages . . . Built them right in the middle of a swamp.
VONNE: *(To GABE)* Your friend is a good talker.
GABE: Heard him argue black is white. He should have been a priest.
LOUIS: People still living in the shacks by the lake . . . cottages buckling, sinking into muskeg. Goddamn it, what the hell. I lost my train of thought.
VONNE: How the Indians got screwed.
LOUIS: That's right!
VONNE: How the Metis got screwed.
LOUIS: That's right!
VONNE: Makes a good story sometimes. And sometimes not, of course . . .
GABE: Tell her, Louis . . .
VONNE: How I got screwed, for instance. Very close to dull.
HENRY: We don't have to talk about that, Vonne.

VONNE: It's a party, Henry. Have yourself some fun.

HENRY screams wildly like a Rodeo Cowboy, heaves himself to his feet, picks up his chair and throws it against the wall. In fact he need not do precisely that, but whatever he does, it will be a physical act of more than considerable force.

HENRY: Welcome! Home! Gabie! I want to make a speech.
VONNE: No use looking foolish, Henry.
HENRY: And I will make a speech. Because I remember Gabe. Three years ago. Right here in the beer parlour of the Empress Hotel and I showed him a white man could match him drink for drink.
GABE: Cost you twenty dollars.
HENRY: Cost me forty-five, goddamn it.
LOUIS: By Christ, you know how to have a party.
HENRY: And your friend too. Louis. Welcome to the goddamn Empress Hotel. Welcome to the goddamn Tahiti Room. I'm buying. Drink to Louis.
VONNE: I'll drink to that.
GABE: Louis . . .
LOUIS: I'll have Gabe's beer if he's not going to use it.
GABE: Louis . . .
ROSIE: Tell them yourself, Gabe.
GABE: I spent seven years of my life with the priests, five years with the police and the last three years with Louis. Louis was the only one who taught me anything.
ROSIE: He smells of beer.
GABE: Yeah, well, he's better when he's sober.
ROSIE: He's like my father. Norbert and Louis. Drunks.
GABE: Tell her what we're going to do, Louis.
LOUIS: I'm going to have another beer.
GABE: Sure. And then what?
LOUIS: We'll drink. We'll talk . . .
GABE: And when we stop talking.
LOUIS: I never stop talking.
GABE: There's more to do than talking.
LOUIS: Gabe's beating drum for me. Going to set me up as a circuit preacher. Going from place to place. Gathering people together . . . Going to tell them all about Louis . . .
HENRY: Riel!
LOUIS: . . . the one who led the old North-West Rebellion in 1885. And his general, of course, Dumont.
GABE: Don't joke about it.

LOUIS: Dumont, of course, he was the hero. He was the fellow could have made it happen. Went to war against paddle wheeling steam boats and the brand-new Gatling gun. Outnumbered. And he treated the Canadian army like he was hunting it for game.
GABE: And he didn't make it happen.
LOUIS: Yeah. Well, he listened to Riel too long, I guess. Crazy Louis. Watching visions. Talking crazy.
GABE: What's so crazy about Louis Riel?
VONNE: Give Gabe a beer.
GABE: I don't want a beer.
VONNE: Sure you do. Get him a beer, Rosie.
GABE: I'm talking to Louis.
LOUIS: And Louis has five years of drinking to catch up on. Last night I was really drunk was the night I went to jail. Whole of the Queens Beer Parlour tried to raise bail for me but it didn't seem like such a good idea when they got the money on the table. Drank it up instead. Can't say I wouldn't have done the same.
GABE: Louis Riel was going to save the world. Is that crazy?
LOUIS: Yeah.
GABE: Louis Riel didn't spend much time in the Empress Hotel spinning stories with a half-wit and a broken down rodeo rider.
HENRY: Who are you calling a half-wit?
GABE: Shut up, Henry.
HENRY: He's only kidding. He always jokes around like that.
LOUIS: *(A little dangerous)* Who are you calling a broken down rodeo rider.
ROSIE: He's a straight speaker, Gabie. But he's hard to take sometimes.
LOUIS: He's saying I talk about being out of jail when I'm in jail and I talk about being in jail when I'm out. There's a lot of truth in that. Makes you think.
HENRY: Never had any sense, Gabie.
VONNE: Probably stole every car for forty miles around at least once.
HENRY: Never did anything with them except run them through fences.
VONNE: Probably broke down every fence for forty miles around at least once.
HENRY: I remember my brother got right sick of it. Putting up fences so that Gabe could knock them down.
GABE: You got very little else to remember, Henry. Save what your brother thought and what I did.
HENRY: He thought he'd teach him a lesson and when the hotel closed one night, he and some of his boys were waiting outside and Gabe came out sure enough and took off and Charles and his boys took off . . .

86

GABE: I heard all Henry's stories. Fifty times.
HENRY: And Gabe was tearing across the open country like the world was flat. But when he got to our section, he drove right up to a gate and opened it. Drove through. Got out. Closed the gate again. Well, Charles had to laugh . . .
ROSIE: Will you be like them? When you're older?
GABE: How?
ROSIE: You know . . . sitting around every night, getting crazy drunk.
GABE: Why you asking?
ROSIE: Why are you growing your hair so long?
GABE: Rosie is growing up smart ass.
ROSIE: Well, she's growing up.
GABE: You got plans for me? You and your drunken friends?
ROSIE: Why are your pants so tight?

VONNE gooses him.

GABE: Fuck off, Vonne! Fuck off, everybody!
LOUIS: Gabe is going to have himself a little trouble, readjusting.
GABE: Not planning to.
LOUIS: Straight out of jail, back home where there's pretty girls and beer. That's an adjustment. Your parole office will tell you about that.
GABE: Girls and beer got nothing to do with it.
LOUIS: That's where you're wrong. That's where a man of experience has got it all over the young fellows.
GABE: I did enough thinking these three years to know who I am.
LOUIS: Reading classic comic books, true west adventures and the junior encyclopedia.
GABE: Listening to you.
LOUIS: There's your first mistake.
GABE: I don't switch on and off . . .
VONNE: Have a drink, Gabe.
GABE: . . . like a cheap hotel neon sign.
LOUIS: It's a party, isn't it? Take Rosie off somewhere and keep her warm.
GABE: Rosie and I got other things to do.
HENRY: Not Rosie.
GABE: *(To HENRY)* You, shut up!
HENRY: She's been waiting for you.
GABE: You'd stop pimping her and just get stupid drunk, I'd be happier.
HENRY: *(Takes ROSIE's arm)* She likes to dance, Rosie does.
GABE: Leave her alone.
VONNE: Gabe's haywire.

87

GABE: I told you, hands off, Henry.

VONNE: *(To LOUIS)* Time to get under the table. Want to come?

HENRY: The girls are better in the dark and nothing else has changed, right, Gabe?

GABE: It's beer. Vonne throwing her ass around. Rosie on her back. There's nothing else for you.

VONNE: What's wrong with that?

HENRY: I'm dancing with Rosie.

GABE: You got no call to touch her.

HENRY: Try and stop me.

GABE: Going to get your brother in?

HENRY: I don't need old Charles. Not to work you over.

GABE: Step right up, Henry.

HENRY: Who you pushing?

VONNE: *(To LOUIS)* Last time he tried to break down the wall with him.

GABE: I'm not joking, Vonne.

ROSIE: You bring your friend home. Louis. Ask us to meet him. Have a party. First thing you know you got Henry laid out on the floor. Nothing funny about that.

VONNE: What's your friend going to think of us?

GABE: Who cares?

VONNE: You do, Gabie.

ROSIE: Sure you do.

LOUIS: You're a scrappy bastard, aren't you?

GABE: I don't take this kind of shit.

LOUIS: Keeps things lively.

GABE: I don't take any shit.

LOUIS: Give it out but you don't take it.

GABE: Meaning?

LOUIS: Tell Henry you aren't going to beat him, Gabe.

GABE: You got the brains of a rabbit, Henry. People with more sense have to keep telling you how to behave.

HENRY: You aren't known for sense.

GABE: Ask Louis then. Ask the big talker. He's got horse sense, common sense, savvy like your goddamn big brother Charles . . . You aren't going to find him up shit creek without a paddle and if you ask him he will tell you to sit there, to keep drinking and stay out of my way . . .

HENRY: You don't know your ass from your elbow.

GABE: You're an animal. There's nothing in your head but fucking and eating and drinking and sleeping.

VONNE: So what?

HENRY: What's wrong with Gabe?

GABE: Tell him, Louis. Where we're going. Why he's moving on.

LOUIS: I talk about being out of jail when I'm in jail and being in jail when I'm out.

GABE: Will you shove that crap?

LOUIS: And jail is going to change a person.

GABE: Not me.

LOUIS: Me for instance. They took an idle, good-for-nothing half-breed and they taught me a trade.

GABE: I haven't changed.

LOUIS: Taught me how to make car licence plates.

GABE: Useful.

LOUIS: I'm a machinist.

GABE: You're a drunken, jailbird half-breed.

LOUIS: Give him a beer.

HENRY: The thing about Gabie is, he's got to be yelling all the time.

LOUIS: Lively, goddamn it. Used to yell myself.

GABE: Why does the whole town come out and start drinking with you? Why are you the hero? Because you talk so fine. Like you talked to me. Day after day. I'm a prisoner because I'm a Metis. I'm a political prisoner from the lost Metis nation.

LOUIS: You're a good listener.

GABE: You've stopped talking.

LOUIS: The beer is talking.

GABE: Goddamn it, Louis. We might as well be where we're supposed to be, sucking a tit at the parole office. Talk is shit, Louis. Nothing is happening.

VONNE: And we'll drink to the Metis nation.

GABE: You aren't a political prisoner.

LOUIS: Drink to Louis Riel.

GABE: You went to jail because you got pissed, you put your fist through a store window and you beat up a mounted policeman.

VONNE: Where Gabe got polluted and hot-wired a car.

GABE: Break and enter. Assault and battery. Auto theft.

LOUIS: You got to wonder why every young Indian, every young half-breed at P.A. got drunk enough once in his life to think he could drive some farmer's truck through a tree.

GABE: I'm wondering what you're going to do about it.

LOUIS: Help you look for Louis Riel. Come on. Where is the bastard. Time he bought a round.

GABE: I am not looking, Louis. I am here. At Batoche.

LOUIS: Getting bigger and bigger and badder and badder . . .

GABE: Bravest, toughest, smartest . . .

LOUIS: Indian cowboys. Win both ways.

GABE: Why not?

LOUIS: Dance hall girls. Prairie sunsets.

GABE: Seen it all.

LOUIS: Sell tickets to you.
GABE: Three fifty. Five dollars. Hell.
LOUIS: Northern lights. Gopher holes. Big black hats. Cinema-scope.
GABE: Goddamn right, you son-of-a-bitch.
LOUIS: Three more hours in the Empress Hotel, you'll be larger than life . . .
GABE: I don't need the Empress Hotel.
LOUIS: By Jesus, I don't think you do.
HENRY: Gabe wants some excitement.
LOUIS: Why not?
GABE: Why not?
HENRY: You want to go through town raising hell.
GABE: Damn right.
HENRY: You've done that before, boy.
GABE: Don't call me boy.
HENRY: Gabie boy is playing he's a man.

GABE knocks HENRY out of his seat. He laughs.

GABE: Oh, those are fighting words, Henry. I heard nothing like that from you since you were fourteen. You called my mother a whore then sicked old Charles on me.
HENRY: I didn't say I wanted to fight.
GABE: I heard what you said.
HENRY: I didn't mean nothing with it.
GABE: Well, you don't have to worry, Henry, because I've been reformed and revised and rehabilitated. I'm an unabridged, unaggressive pacifist, Henry. I been born again, I seen the light. That's the Canadian prison system for you, Henry. They take a no good half-breed rough-neck and they put him in the chapel every Sunday, since there's nowhere else to go and I saw God, Henry. God is where Vonne is going to take you, if she stops laughing long enough. Glory be to the Father and to the Son and to the Holy Ghost, Henry. God told me that I shouldn't fight you, no matter how goddamn stupid you were. *(He makes the sign of the cross on HENRY's forehead, using his beer as holy water)* Lets pray together, Henry.

He pours the rest of the beer over HENRY's head.

HENRY: Leave go of me.
GABE: What do we want down here on our knees, Henry? We're looking for God. And if we find the bugger, we'll ask him for what you want most in the whole world. What's that, Henry? Another round of Molson Ex, good friends standing by you, Vonne, where

90

you can get her easy enough. That's for you, Henry. And I want Louis Riel who fought at Batoche when that was somewhere to be.
VONNE: And what does Louis Riel want?
GABE: Metis rights!

> *GABE walks away from HENRY who tries to make a joke of it.*

HENRY: Gabe was always good at stories. Hah. We'd be tracking things through the bush. Gabe saying he could live in the bush for six months without his rifle, without his pocket knife, Gabie making snowshoes . . .
GABE: I remember I tied you up in your barn and left you, Henry. I guess Charles got you free.
HENRY: He needs some help. *(Pause)* Charles.
GABE: The whole family's in a bad way, my friend.
HENRY: At the gas station. *(To LOUIS)* He needs a machinist. *(To GABE)* And a pump jockey.
GABE: Your brother runs a one-man garage.
HENRY: He wants to expand.
GABE: He's losing more money than a dirt farmer now. Only way he can expand is to hire me and Louis. Because a half-breed gets minimum wage to do the mule work.
HENRY: He's got some things he wants fixed up. Couple of weeks work anyway.
GABE: And you put him up to it. Didn't you, Henry?
HENRY: He wants to expand. Charles.
GABE: Gets pretty lonely out there on the highway. Nothing to do but jerk yourself off. Henry's always liked me. Followed me around. Since we were boys.
HENRY: You're not working, Gabe.
GABE: No.
HENRY: Don't know how much opportunity you think there is around here . . .
GABE: A man wants to work, not afraid of getting dirty, he can dig in, put down roots, make a good life for himself, isn't that true?
HENRY: Not around here, Gabe.
GABE: Doesn't worry me. I expect any day now, some big record company executive is going to drive through here in a yellow Lincoln convertible, going to discover me singing by the side of the road and make me a star.
VONNE: Why don't you try pumping gas? If big cars impress you.
GABE: You're very understanding.
VONNE: Rosie's working. In the hotel dining-room.
GABE: I don't give a good goddamn.
ROSIE: Gabie won't give a good goddamn about half the time. The other half he doesn't give a fuck.

HENRY: Norbert's land is up for taxes.

GABE: Leave me, Henry.

HENRY: So you can't work for him, I mean.

GABE: I know what you mean.

HENRY: If Charles wrote a letter. To the parole office. Said you turned down a job.

GABE: You make me real tired, Henry.

LOUIS: Heard about a high steel gang in Cedar Rapids. You hear about that Vonne? Danger pay. Only good Indian's the one that's falling from the forty-ninth floor.

HENRY: I'd like it. If you took the job. There's things to do. There's more than I can handle.

GABE: That's enough.

LOUIS: Easy, Gabe.

GABE: You ever stop to think that what a man can buy for two fifty an hour isn't much of a challenge . . . Try a little harder.

HENRY: That's good money, Gabie, around here . . .

GABE: How much do you make?

HENRY: I got responsibilities.

GABE: You will have if you take us on.

HENRY: It's a start, isn't it? And nobody is going to pay you for living off the bush, are they?

GABE: The thing is, Henry, you got to realize, you're not buying a "pump jockey," you're buying a friend. Two friends. What's that worth, Henry?

HENRY: Working at the gas station could be a hell of a lot better than going back to jail.

GABE: But you aren't talking like a friend . . .

LOUIS: What they're building in Cedar Rapids . . .

GABE: You're talking like a soul-saving, do-gooder, social worker. Taking trouble making work for two worthless half-breeds on parole.

LOUIS: It's the tallest, highest, biggest, baddest insurance company in the world. Wouldn't that be something. Working up there, right against the sky?

HENRY: Going to jail is what is going to happen if the parole board finds you turning down work.

> *LOUIS has been trying to keep GABE off HENRY's throat. HENRY doesn't seem to realize he's talking too much. LOUIS gives him up as a lost cause and lets GABE loose.*

GABE: You want your boots licked? You want your ass kissed? You want me to take this fucking job? What do you want me to do first?

LOUIS: He's saying he needs time to think.
VONNE: Ha.
GABE: Think! You know what I think . . .?
LOUIS: Shut up, Gabe!
GABE: Stoney Mountain is one kind of jail. Jackson's Super
Shell Service Station is another kind of jail. Stoney Mountain costs
you more and I think if you're planning on keeping me in jail, it's
going to cost you.
ROSIE: I start at two.

She gets up. GABE grabs her arm.

GABE: Rosie always had ambitions. Waiting table . . .
ROSIE: Washing dishes . . .
GABE: Whatever. Respectable. Not so rewarding as Vonne there,
turning tricks, but it's steady. Isn't that right?
ROSIE: It's real dull, Gabe.

She exits.

GABE: Then stay here, honey.
VONNE: *(Calling after her)* It's the beer talking, Rosie.
GABE: I'm not drinking. Louis. He's the drunken no-good. I'm
the smart ass punk.
HENRY: Rosie wants you to take the job.
GABE: She knows where she can stuff it.
VONNE: Louis doesn't need your job, Henry. He's going to work
in high steel construction.
LOUIS: Right across the border as if it wasn't there. Vonne's
coming with me.
GABE: And you can shut up about Cedar Rapids.
VONNE: When I get to Cedar Rapids, I'm going to start all over
as a call girl.
GABE: I'll kill you, Louis.
LOUIS: We're going to build our own high steel project right
here in Batoche.
GABE: Damn right.
LOUIS: Going to transmit from the top of it. To our Metis
brothers.
GABE: That's right.
LOUIS: Going to generate the power. Going to stay here in
Batoche. Going to get a job stake together.
VONNE: *(With wonder)* Gabie's taking Henry's job.
HENRY: I just want to help, Gabe.
GABE: I don't need your help.
HENRY: Well, sure you do . . .

GABE: Why, Henry?
HENRY: Should be thanking me and Charles . . .
GABE: Why, Henry?
HENRY: Like I said, there's not much work around here . . .
GABE: Why, Henry?
HENRY: And you're half-breeds, aren't you?
GABE: You know what he wants, Louis? Take that coil of rope
and pipe it up to the ceiling. Like *Astounding Tales*. Like some
Hindu mystical medicine-man. Climb up the rope and disappear.
That would be an Indian rope trick with some point to it.
HENRY: I want you to come and work for me.
GABE: Wouldn't it be easy if we just disappeared. Turn white for
him, Louis.
HENRY: I just want you to go to work.
GABE: Jesus, Henry, you are really something.
HENRY: It's the night shift. I run the station at night.
GABE: Sure you do, Henry. Sitting up all night with nothing to
do, that's about as far as your abilities stretch. But now you got
two half-breeds on parole. So you can sit out on that highway
with two half-breeds working for you.
HENRY: I don't hold a grudge, Gabe.
GABE: I read comic books . . .
HENRY: Well, hell, so do I!
GABE: . . . with heroes who can turn into rubber, into plastic.
Bullet proof guys. People can fly.
HENRY: We write the comic books, you know. You're not so
goddamn smart. Goddamn white man writes the goddamn comic
books.

> *HENRY leaves and GABE shouts after him, before*
> *storming out in the opposite direction.*

GABE: . . . Mounties with sled dogs just as smart as they are.
These are the guys I know about. You want me invisible, you're
going to put up with this invisible bastard, laughing at you. You
can't see him, but he's there.
VONNE: Watching Gabie is exhausting.
LOUIS: He'll take Henry's job.
VONNE: So I see.
LOUIS: So don't worry about him. If you want to make him feel
better just tell him how Louis Riel told Sir John A. MacDonald
that he was the pope of the fucking new world.
VONNE: Is that all?
LOUIS: Tell him how Gabriel Dumont took some spent cartridges
and a silver arrow out in the bush. Then he captured three regiments
of the Canadian Army, including the Prince Albert volunteers. I
made that one up.

VONNE: Gabriel Dumont trained the birds off the trees. Charmed the birds and the bees.
LOUIS: And the loaves and the fishes. Christ, he's better than church.

In the parking lot or field behind the hotel, GABE sings to himself. ROSIE enters during the song.

GABE: *(Sings)*
I gave my girl friend a transistor radio
She cuts me off all day
I gave my girl friend a transistor radio
She cuts me off all day
I got a girl friend who's wired to the sound
Of a country and western deejay.

I took my girl friend out in the country
I meant to find us some hay
I took my girl friend out in the country
I meant to find us some hay
Her batteries went dead and she heard what I said
I said let's go to bed
She laid shit on my head.

I gave you a transistor radio
I did not count the cost
I gave you a transistor radio
I did not count the cost
We can both plug in so let's begin
But we got our wires crossed.

ROSIE: Thought you were up on your soap box.
GABE: Passing through, Rosie. Wouldn't want to bore you.
ROSIE: Everyone for forty miles around thinks you and I are going to settle down. Except you.
GABE: Rosie reading movie magazines and true confessions. Amadee Forget falling down drunk all over you and you're watching the ceiling with bubble gum music in your head.
ROSIE: You don't know what I'm thinking.
GABE: Sure I do. You think I'm something. You think I'm getting out of Batoche and I'm going to take you with me. You think you're going to have a house with one bedroom for us and one for the girls and one for the boys. And those little boys and girls are going to get tucked up in their little white sheets. And you and I are going to be screwing around all night. On black satin sheets. They sell those in the movie magazines, don't they?
ROSIE: *(Laughing)* Doesn't have to be black.

GABE: And I'll be so tired I'll hardly make it down to somebody else's service station. You got very romantic ideas, Rosie.

ROSIE: You been talking to Kenny Mitchell.

GABE: They been talking to me, sweet little girl, but that's not what they're saying. Kenny says you damn near froze his ass to the dashboard of McQuarrie's pick up truck.

ROSIE: I damn near killed him.

GABE: So he told me.

ROSIE: Because I had no more vouchers for panty hose and how am I going to explain that to the Welfare.

GABE: Yeah, I heard that.

ROSIE: Gabe?

GABE: What?

ROSIE: Did you ask Kenny about me?

GABE: Yes.

ROSIE: Were you mad?

GABE: Why would I be mad?

ROSIE: Why did you ask him?

GABE: What am I supposed to do? I come back here, first thing I understand is Norbert's daughter, Rosie, is all set up for me, not that anybody except Rosie thinks that's a good idea. So all of them are making sure I hear about Kenny Mitchell and the long cold winter when there's nothing else to do.

ROSIE: You know a lot of girls.

GABE: I've been in jail for three years, Rosie. I got political instead.

ROSIE: You used to know a lot of girls.

GABE: Yeah.

ROSIE: When you went to jail, that was because of a woman.

GABE: Like I said, you got very romantic ideas.

ROSIE: You got drunk because those two cowboys beat up a girl you knew.

GABE: I don't need an excuse to get drunk.

ROSIE: But you had one.

GABE: I love women. I love talking and women and everything that takes all your mind and your time. Everything except Jackson's gas station, which is not a consuming interest.

ROSIE: Are you leaving?

GABE: Nothing going around here.

ROSIE: Louis is here.

GABE: Talking in the beer parlour.

ROSIE: You like talking.

GABE: More than you can fathom, is it?

ROSIE: Maybe.

GABE: Talking when it takes all my mind. Talking when I care about it. Just talking, I get tired. Why not? I've been talking crazy since I got here and now I'm sitting here like my father's beside me and a hundred ghosts, making some kind of holy agreement with them. I won't talk again. What's the use of talking. What else is there to do?

ROSIE: Did you miss me? While you were gone?

GABE: You're a pretty girl, Rosie.

ROSIE: Did you miss me?

GABE: No.

ROSIE: Crazy bastard.

GABE: I don't need people.

ROSIE: Save for Louis.

GABE: And I don't need him for damn sure. Not when he's sitting around like you and Henry Jackson. Living in some happy time when I lead you and Vonne and Henry out of the wilderness.

ROSIE: Crazy bastard.

GABE: I don't need the wilderness. I'd rather steal cars, Rosie. Or set fires.

ROSIE: For your Metis brothers.

GABE: It could be.

ROSIE: Why don't you go to Regina and sit in the lobby of the Parliament Buildings. Why don't you sit on top of the Parliament Buildings? You look like you got a steeple up your ass.

> *ROSIE walks into the area representing Jackson's Service Station as HENRY and VONNE enter.*

HENRY: Now, I want you girls to hide. No. You're not both getting behind that gas pump. You're sticking out, girls. Quiet, they're coming. Quit giggling, Vonne. *(As he turns up his radio)* Giggle over that, goddamn it.

> *LOUIS joins GABE.*

LOUIS: Henry Jackson has a new transistor radio.

GABE: He has a credit rating.

LOUIS: Because he works for his brother and his brother's gas station puts four men to work. Man with that kind of business is the foundation of the community.

GABE: How's business, Henry?

LOUIS: Who's that giggling?

GABE: What's Vonne doing behind the gas pump?

HENRY: Got a visitor dropped by to see you.

VONNE: Two visitors.

HENRY: You aren't visiting, Ee-vonne. You make this place feel homey.

GABE: Rosie. Oh, Christ.

97

ROSIE: Keeps things lively.

LOUIS: Better late than never, Henry. Here's the graveyard shift.

GABE: *(To ROSIE)*   You got nothing better to do than hang around a grease pit?

ROSIE: Dish washing. Beer drinking.

GABE: Why are you following me around all the time? Want me to teach you how to pump gas? Want to crawl under a car with me?

ROSIE: How about a grease job?

HENRY is following LOUIS, brandishing a sheaf of paper.

HENRY: I've been working on some plans. Renovations.

LOUIS takes one sheet of paper and glances at it. The rest of the papers escape him and drift to the floor.

LOUIS: Let's see them, Henry.

HENRY: Got the idea out of *Popular Mechanics*. Where's the one I want here . . .

GABE has picked up a piece of the paper and glances at it idly.

GABE: Jesus, Henry, this looks more like a cat-house than a gas station.

HENRY: *(To LOUIS)*   That's the front view. That's from the side road. Shows the new outbuilding. That's like a floor plan. From up above.

LOUIS: You been working on this all day?

HENRY: All week.

LOUIS: Think the trade will justify it?

HENRY: Sure it will.

GABE: Why don't you stand here and copy down the licence numbers, all the cars that go by. Be a more practical project.

HENRY: *(To LOUIS)*   See this is the sales room like a before picture and this is the after . . . Must have dropped the after.

LOUIS: A lot of work gone into those plans.

HENRY: *(Eagerly)*   Once I started, couldn't stop. See here's the partition here now. Got to move the map rack.

GABE: Something obscene about the way you draw a gas pump.

LOUIS: Once Gabe starts, he just can't stop.

VONNE: Rosie came down here to see you, Gabe.

GABE: If she thinks I've got anything like these gas pumps, she's in for a surprise.

LOUIS: Gabie's got his sleeves rolled up. Let's get to work.
HENRY: I thought we could have a party. Well, sure because we don't get much business on the week-end. Vonne helped me plan it, didn't you, Vonne? There's music. And I bought some whiskey.
VONNE: I'm drinking this whiskey.
HENRY: Well, there's more. Sure. Because Friday night everyone stays in town, you see, and there might not be a car out here from one end of the shift to the other. Not unless we ask them to deliver Chinese food. Ha. *(But no one seems to think that's funny and no one wants Chinese food either)* Well, I'd like to make a toast. Like to welcome you, Gabe, and also Louis, to Jackson's Service Station.

VONNE and ROSIE cheer.

VONNE: Says what he means and he means what he says.
ROSIE: And he's buying again.
VONNE: Ray. Ray. Ray.
HENRY: What do you think of that?

Pause.

LOUIS: *(Finally)* It's kind of you, Henry. Isn't it, Gabe?
GABE: You're a prince, Henry.
HENRY: Now it wasn't all my idea. No. It was Vonne, too. Wanted to make sure you got the right kind of welcome, didn't you, Vonne?
VONNE: *(Grown unaccountably shy)* The thing about Henry's radio, it has this plug here, you can stick it in your ear.

She does, and starts to dance.

HENRY: I told her, Vonne, a gas station, it doesn't seem to be much for a party atmosphere and she told me that it was having your friends around you made a party, even if all you were doing was passing a bottle around in a circle at the side of the road.
GABE: All we are doing Henry.
LOUIS: *(To HENRY, but for GABE's benefit)* Nights like this, with your friends around you. Makes it all worthwhile.
HENRY: *(To LOUIS)* Something I wanted to talk to you about.
LOUIS: What?
HENRY: You and Vonne should get together.
GABE: Vonne's all wired up to your transistor radio.
ROSIE: Shut up, Gabe.
HENRY: *(To LOUIS)* You should ask her to dance or something.
GABE: She's dancing. She don't need encouragement.

99

HENRY: *(To LOUIS)* Go on. Ask her.
LOUIS: No, I couldn't do that.
HENRY: Go on. She likes you.
GABE: Oh, Christ.
LOUIS: I thought you and Vonne . . .
HENRY:. She likes you.
GABE: Oh, Christ.
LOUIS: *(To HENRY)* You think so?
GABE: I think this whole goddamn thing is crazy. *(To LOUIS)* Where do you think you're going?
LOUIS: Dance with Vonne.
GABE: She's a three fifty ticket or a big wide smile. You know that, Louis.
LOUIS: Fuck off!
GABE: Well, I had enough of your party, Henry . . .
LOUIS: Vonne?
GABE: Vonne is bouncing up and down, saying she likes country music when it's just her pants are hot.
LOUIS: *(To HENRY)* She's not listening.
GABE: *(To HENRY)* And the whiskey's rotgut.
HENRY: Well, there's more. Hell.
GABE: And Rosie's watching me as if that passed the time.
LOUIS: *(To himself)* Well, why not then?
GABE: Because it's embarrassing, Louis.
LOUIS: *(To VONNE)* Vonne, well, I thought . . .
VONNE: *(Jumping in)* What?
LOUIS: *(Awkward)* I'm beginning to like you. When's your birthday. Ha.

GABE sings. LOUIS and VONNE dance.

GABE: *(Sings)*
I met a man who said to me
The Metis nation's proud and free
And you and me can show them what to be
I felt the glory, seen the light
But I end up here every night
Eating shit and bored out of my tree.

I should have known it wasn't true
In fact I guess I know I knew
I knew that I had heard his con before
He's a rodeo rider who forgot his horse
And he don't have much to do of course
Save for jumping on and off a two-bit whore.

100

HENRY loves the song. He sings the second verse again. GABE cuffs him hard enough to knock him over.

GABE: You're so stupid, Henry.
HENRY: You're kidding, aren't you?
GABE: What do you think?
HENRY: Haywire smart ass bastard.
ROSIE: Just leave him.
HENRY: Gone too far.
LOUIS: Leave him, Henry.
GABE: What she wants you to do, Louis, is tear the goddamn radio off her ear, rip her blouse open. Back her up against a wall somewhere so Henry can watch.
LOUIS: Leave me, Gabe.
HENRY: He wants a fight, he's asking for it.
LOUIS: No, he isn't.
HENRY: I'll fight him for you.
VONNE: *(With the transistor radio)* Take this, Henry. Stick it in your ear.
LOUIS: He wants a few speeches. A few fine thoughts.
GABE: More than that.
LOUIS: Gabe's very bright. Managed to go through eight years of church school without finding that out. Used to ask questions and the answers weren't in the books. Got his knuckles rapped.
GABE: Beat me for it.
LOUIS: Out of school with nothing to do but get in trouble. Finally made three years worth of trouble. Met me. I'm a rodeo hero, used to putting on a great amount of style. Gabe was listening . . . he had too much time to think . . . you remember what I told you?
GABE: I'll kill you, Louis.
LOUIS: I told him things he could be proud of. How the Indians lived before the whites came and about their ideas of property, how property was held in common. And I told him what I thought that private ownership did to people. That some people had and others had not. And that set-up can get kind of like a jail outside a jail, so pretty soon people can be born and live and die, having not, and their children the same. I gave him a lot of attention. He misses it. He's jealous, Vonne. Don't notice him.
GABE: You bastard!
LOUIS: I've been in jail a lot and I talk a lot in jail to pass the time. Because the conversation is not so stimulating in the ordinary way.
GABE: You come out of P.A. just to lie here dying.

101

LOUIS: You think you've got the answers now. You want to be a circuit riding preacher and you want me to carry your cross.
GABE: I do, yes.
LOUIS: I've done the circuit breaking wild horses. I've had it.
GABE: What's the use of talking?
LOUIS: I think I made more money than you'll ever see. All off the rodeos. And I spent it all living higher than you'll ever want to . . . than I hope you'll ever want to. Almost killed myself spending it. I got myself drunk as a skunk on very old special brandy, drove my great big yellow convertible off a bridge into the mighty Saskatchewan River. Got out of hospital to find my luck was gone. Well, the big car was gone. I was still as big and brave as hell but I didn't win anymore. Ended up as a rodeo clown, running for a barrel. Quite a figure of fun. The money was not so good. The drinking was bad. So I stopped it. I got no intention of starting over. What do you think of that?
GABE: I think you're talking fine again. Talking poetry. Talking pretty. Talking shit.
LOUIS: It's not so much what you say, it's how you say it and if you say it so it sounds good enough, there's people going to believe it. You should leave off telling stories. Since you end up lying to yourself. You should try and learn a trade.

GABE picks up HENRY's whiskey bottle.

GABE: You know what I think? I think I can finish this bottle in one swallow. Want to bet, Louis? Watch me.
LOUIS: No need to go that far.
ROSIE: Gabie drinks like a kid.

GABE drains the bottle. The others watch.

GABE: By Christ, you're all looking at me like I was a bomb. Exploding. By Jesus. I see why you do it, Louis. Why you're drinking all the time.
LOUIS: Not your style.
GABE: You don't know my style.
LOUIS: You're not a drinker.
GABE: Henry will listen to you. Vonne will listen to you. Because they are shit heads. They got nothing else to do.
VONNE: Vonne is drinking.
GABE: So am I, Vonne.

He takes VONNE's bottle.

VONNE: Just shove it up your ass, Gabe.

102

LOUIS: Leave it!
GABE: Leave me!
LOUIS: Goddamn kid! All right!

(LOUIS leaves)

GABE: Watch me, Rosie. I can finish this one too.
ROSIE: *(Exits)* I've seen that done, Gabe.
GABE: You've seen nothing!
HENRY: Yippee, Gabie!
VONNE: Shut up, Henry.
HENRY: You see that? That's the second bottle he's got there.
Isn't that something?
VONNE: Thought you were going to beat him for me?
HENRY: By Jesus, I wouldn't go near him. I seen him crazy
drunk before.
VONNE: You can wait till he falls over and kick him a little.
HENRY: I seen him drunk but I never seen him so drunk as he's
getting right now.
VONNE: Maybe he'll rush the gas station, Henry. Maybe you
should plan on holding him off.
HENRY: Where's he gone? Where is he?

*In fact, GABE has wandered off with the remains of
the bottle.*

VONNE: Right behind you.
HENRY: What? Shit, Vonne, no, he isn't. Say . . .
VONNE: What?
HENRY: You remember what happened when Charles got hold
of that dog of Gabe's, used to follow him round. That orange dog.
The one that pissed in Charles' hat that time.
VONNE: Good-bye, Henry.
HENRY: Vonne?

*HENRY trails out after VONNE as GABE and ROSIE
enter through the hotel to the exterior area at the
rear of the hotel.*

ROSIE: Henry doesn't know what you're talking about.
GABE: When?
ROSIE: When you tell him how stupid he is. If he did know, he'd
kill you.
GABE: Henry's a white man with mush in his head. He thinks
that makes him a full scale Indian.
ROSIE: So do you.

103

GABE: Sure.

ROSIE: You think it's special being Indian. Sure there's a whole government department set up for you, but they're white, they don't know what they're doing. They don't understand you at all. They don't know how drunk you can get and they don't know how stupid you can be.

GABE: And you think just because a couple of nuns taught you how to run an adding machine, you're going to be a guiding light for the check-out girls at an IGA store in Saskatoon.

ROSIE: *(Laughs)* I do not.

GABE: Shit, Rosie, next thing you'll be telling me you want to go to teacher's college.

This ROSIE finds terribly funny. GABE is not amused.

ROSIE: Next thing I'll say I want to be a nun.

GABE: Sure. You want out of here and you want me to take you out. I'm a half-breed. I've got white blood and it shows, doesn't it? I don't look greasy, do I? Catch me in a dim light, I might not be Indian at all.

ROSIE: You play the part real well.

GABE: Meaning?

ROSIE: You act like you're the band chief looking for the last buffalo.

GABE: I know what I am.

ROSIE: What are you cleaning that gun for?

GABE: It's my gun. It should be clean.

ROSIE: You're on parole.

GABE: I'm going hunting.

ROSIE: You're on parole. You work at Jackson's Gas Station.

GABE: Jesus, you do. You sound like a little white school-teacher, you know that.

ROSIE: I dont . . .

GABE: I'm sick of it. I'm sick of Jackson's Gas Station and I'm sick of you following me around and I'm going out in the bush. I'm going to stay there till I got some peace again and Jackson's not going to do anything about it. The parole board's not going to send me back. Because I'm just another crazy Indian. They locked up all the crazy Indians, they'd have no place to build hockey rinks.

As GABE exits, the lights come up on Jackson's Service Station. HENRY, VONNE and LOUIS enter, ROSIE joins them.

HENRY: Well, if he's going off, I'll tell you one thing. I'm not holding his job open for him. We got to get them renovations finished. Yes sir, first person who comes out here, looking for work, the job's theirs if they want it. If they're qualified.

LOUIS: Gabe's got the qualifications.

HENRY: Well, he's handy.

ROSIE: He used to stay with us young kids when my mother and father went off. Drinking. Two, three days at a time. One time it was three weeks, but I was older then and I think that was after . . . no, that was the same summer Gabie went haywire . . . His mother thought she was something. She kept her looks. She looked like Gabie's sister, last time I remember her. He don't know who his father was.

HENRY: He's too wild.

ROSIE: I don't remember him like that. I remember him telling the little kids stories, comic book stories, but he'd make them up and I was the oldest girl.

HENRY: He only stayed around you because his ma was off to Regina, wearing silver slippers. You'd be better off with me, Rosie, if I'd have you.

VONNE: She don't want you, Henry. You're simple.

HENRY: Gabe won't have her. The thing about that bastard is, he's got women flying over him, taking leaps at him. That Kennedy's wife thinks he's a hell of a stud. She's been driving their Chevy six miles down here so Gabe can top off the gas tank, she'll make it six miles back. Give Rosie a drink, Louis.

LOUIS passes ROSIE the bottle.

LOUIS: It's okay, Henry's got another twenty-sixer in the truck.

HENRY: He ever tell you how he came to steal that car? That was another woman. He hardly knew her. There was a fight outside the beer parlour. Two greasers pulled her into the car.

VONNE: We want to stop talking about Gabe all the time.

HENRY: Two mounties standing there laughing. Gabe took off after them. He's got a mind of his own but he was totalled and he totalled the car, of course.

VONNE: You will understand, Henry, that Louis and I got better things to do.

HENRY: Well, sure. Keeps things lively.

VONNE: Isn't that right, Louis?

LOUIS: I guess I told him up to thirty, forty times, all about the North-West Rebellion, all about the rodeo.

VONNE: Isn't that right, Louis. You and I are going to have ourselves a time.

LOUIS: God loves his soldiers.

VONNE: Sure he does, honey.
LOUIS: Dumont was a general.
VONNE: What's going on?
LOUIS: *(To ROSIE)*   Did he say where he was going?
ROSIE: To the bush.
LOUIS: Gabe can take care of himself.
ROSIE: He can't stay out of trouble.
VONNE: Sure. He's probably off somewhere right now, shooting a hole through his foot.
ROSIE: I remember Gabie came by one night. Tapping on the window. There was frost in his hair.
LOUIS: Gabe got me to come up here to Batoche with him. He said, it's my town Louis. You can take it over. They'll name it after you.
HENRY: Charles used to beat him up a lot.
ROSIE: Let's have a party.
VONNE: We're having a party.
ROSIE: Get the other bottle.
VONNE: Plenty there still.

ROSIE drains the bottle she's holding.

ROSIE: Get it, Henry.
HENRY: Sure. Why not?
LOUIS: He'll tell you I did the talking. Ha. That's one of his stories.
ROSIE: Frost in his hair. Pushing snow down my back.
HENRY: I guess he could kill Charles now, if he wanted.
ROSIE: It's no good, is it?
LOUIS: Got a mind of his own.
ROSIE: He's supposed to be your friend. He didn't even tell you he was going. Sometimes I could kill him, Louis.
LOUIS: Gone as far as that.
ROSIE: He's gone off because he thinks nobody tells him what to do. Thing is, everyone tells him what to do. He just does the opposite.
LOUIS: He's like you.

A blare of music, loud and tinny, badly amplified.
HENRY returns with another bottle of whiskey.

VONNE: And I think we should have a party.
HENRY: You like that? I got a loudspeaker wired into the radio in the truck.
ROSIE: He doesn't care about me, does he?
HENRY: *Popular Mechanics.*

LOUIS: Sure he does. And we care about you. Little Rosie. Sweet little girl. We care about you a lot.
VONNE: Turn off that radio.
ROSIE: I want to dance.
LOUIS: Sure.
HENRY: Dance with her, Louis.
LOUIS: Well, all right then. Well, watch me.
ROSIE: Dance with me. Watch me. Fuck him.
VONNE: Turn off that radio. Turn off that fucking radio.

> *ROSIE dances, joined by LOUIS. The music and the dance peak. HENRY watches, very intent.*

ROSIE: I don't care about Gabe.
LOUIS: It's okay, honey. It's all right.
VONNE: I didn't come out here to watch you two climbing all over each other.
HENRY: The thing is, Louis, I noticed Wednesday is always a little slow. You got to wait till Friday, if it's a pay-day Friday, to see any traffic at all on this road. I mean, I figure we could knock off for a while, Louis, what do you think. Not up to Gabe to have all the fun, is it? Louis? What do you say? Louis?

> *Blackout.*

Act Two

Lights up on ROSIE and GABE.

ROSIE: So I went to confession. I had Father Paul and he's been looking at you and me sideways ever since you came back. So I surprised him. He pretended he couldn't stop coughing.
GABE: Why did you go to confession?
ROSIE: You have to if you want to take communion.
GABE: Why do you want to take communion?
ROSIE: I don't.
GABE: You're like me, aren't you?
ROSIE: No.
GABE: Sure you are. Whole town watching your middle for signs of my kid and you end up laying out for all talk no action Louis. Just for the shock of it. Rosie, honey, there's something real wrong with your head.
ROSIE: Passes the time.
GABE: Louis taken with you now?
ROSIE: He was drunk.
GABE: Yeah, well, he's always drunk.
ROSIE: I don't even think he remembers.
GABE: Drunk as a skunk in the cab of another pick-up truck and him talking all the whole time while your head is banging on the dashboard. Little Rosie. I guess he told you it was poetry.
ROSIE: Yeah, well, I didn't believe him.
GABE: Why not?
ROSIE: It isn't poetry, is it?
GABE: Poor Rosie.
ROSIE: Why poor Rosie? What do you know?
GABE: I know it's better in bed for one thing.
ROSIE: You know street tramps in Regina!
GABE: I don't like my women so lonely there's nothing else for them to do.
ROSIE: Your women!
GABE: I had women when you were wishing I'd come by and catch frogs with you, Rosie.
ROSIE: You think you know everything.
GABE: Damn near.

109

ROSIE: You don't know so much because you make it all up. Your women. You got all your women dressed in silver paper in your head. Speaking French.

GABE: You going to ask me what happened when I was out in the bush?

ROSIE: No.

GABE: You peddling your ass around, you think that's all that happened?

ROSIE: I didn't peddle . . .

GABE: It's a big country, Rosie. Come on.

ROSIE: No.

GABE: I'm going to tell you. Didn't have a drink for two weeks. That's to satisfy the schoolteacher in you that wants me settled down. That's not the interesting part. I made a fast.

ROSIE: You mean you went hungry.

GABE: I lived off that bush when I was younger and stupider than you'll ever be . . . I mean I didn't eat for two days, almost three . . . just to clear my mind.

ROSIE: What mind?

GABE: There it is. I'm not eating. I haven't spoken for about a week. I'm forcing myself to stay awake, just to see what will happen. This is the third day. The sun is coming up.

A long pause.

ROSIE: What happened?

GABE: I passed out from the weakness. I woke up, my arm was gone right up to the shoulder, down the throat of a hungry looking wolverine.

ROSIE: What happened?

GABE: What happens when you fast, you wouldn't know this, being purely interested in physical pleasures, you have visions. You go right off your skull. The sun came up over the lake. The lake was on fire. There's a voice inside my head, but it's everywhere. Realest thing I ever heard. "Gabe, this is what you're going to do, I'll lay it out for you. This is your destiny." I knew it wasn't me talking then. Destiny is not a word I'd use.

ROSIE: Then what happened?

GABE: Voice kept going.

ROSIE: What did it say?

GABE: I don't know. I was laughing too hard.

ROSIE: Because I guess you think you're very funny.

GABE: No, it's true. The whole story. You know what I mean?

ROSIE: No.

GABE: You care?

ROSIE: No.

110

GABE: You know the only thing that worries me, Rosie? Sometimes I think I'm crazy. My father was some wandering white maniac. With an axe. Sure. He had fits, Rosie. Didn't know what was happening to him.

ROSIE: Norbert's crazy.

GABE: You aren't like Norbert, Rosie. You know it.

ROSIE: My old man is crazier than you could ever think up.

GABE: I'm trying to tell you that I don't know what I'm going to do next. Half the time. That I feel crazy, Rosie. Half the time. And the only thing that I can say about what is going to happen . . . I mean, happen to me . . . it's going to be wild, Rosie, it's going to be crazy.

ROSIE: I feel like that.

GABE: There are words in my head, if I say them, I can't understand why there isn't somebody there to answer back. And sometimes I think I know all the answers. Got the questions and the answers all my own in one head. You can see how crazy that is.

ROSIE: All the things in your head, Gabe, they already happened.

GABE: I guess so.

ROSIE: That's why you think they're so big.

GABE: Sure. Dumont and Riel made it happen. Right? Almost made it happen. And all I do is come back to Batoche.

ROSIE: Louis will be glad you're back.

GABE: Sure. Well, next time, I'll give you a little warning. Take you both with me. Take three things with me. Rosie. Louis. And a hunting knife. What will you take, Rosie?

ROSIE: Black satin sheets.

GABE: What else?

ROSIE: Why are you taking Louis?

GABE: All right. Going out in the bush with two things. Rosie and a hunting knife.

ROSIE: You can take him if you want to.

GABE: Oh, sure. I can go out in the bush with Louis. With Henry. All the white men of the world. All the losers of the world. I could guide them through the wilderness.

ROSIE: You like Louis.

GABE: Or I could do it by myself. I can't depend on Louis all my life, now can I?

Some of which is overheard by LOUIS and VONNE who enter from the Tahiti Room.

LOUIS: There's something we have to settle, Gabe.

GABE: There's something I want to finish telling you, Rosie. What happened when I was out in the bush. I followed Norbert's excuse for a trap-line, mainly. Laughable. When I was young, I lived off Norbert's traps sometimes. He used to have it together. Christ. Well, it's one more thing I'm going to have to learn to do for myself. Right?

VONNE: Louis went hunting on the week-end.

GABE: What did you get, Louis?

LOUIS: Nothing.

VONNE: Rabbit.

LOUIS: Nothing.

VONNE: Bought three rounds at the Empress Hotel on the strength of them.

LOUIS: You know what happened while you were gone.

GABE: Empress sold a lot of beer.

LOUIS: At the gas station.

GABE: Trade was not substantial.

> *LOUIS delivers his next speech as a set piece, a formal apology. It seems to be the protocol of another time. The puncturing of LOUIS's posture satisfies GABE, he is willing to make peace but finds he's gone too far.*

LOUIS: Want you to know, Gabe, that it wouldn't have happened. No. I don't know what to say. I feel kind of bad. I guess I stepped out of line but I don't know what to say about it. Is that all right?

GABE: What do you mean?

LOUIS: Me and Rosie.

GABE: Christ, Louis. Rosie didn't mind.

> *Pause. LOUIS explodes.*

LOUIS: Saskatchewan does not amount to much.

GABE: Uncivilized.

LOUIS: There's other places I could be.

GABE: Well, sure.

LOUIS: Going to Cedar Rapids.

GABE: That's fine, Louis.

LOUIS: Don't believe me, do you?

GABE: Sure I do. Sure. It sounds like a good plan.

LOUIS: You don't think I'm going, do you? You think I'm shit. You think I'm going to stick around this asshole town with your name all over it. Watching you hell around like helling around was going out of style. Like there was a future in it. I've raised more hell than you'll even get a chance to dream about.

GABE: Going to get Henry to sell me a car he's got down at the station. Going to take advantage of his good nature, since he knows what a tough bastard I am. Going to say I'll give him fifty dollars for it, since it ain't worth ten.
LOUIS: I don't suppose you want a beer. You don't see the value of it. You're too good for beer-drinking.
GABE: I don't need it.
LOUIS: I need a beer to stomach you.

LOUIS exits.

GABE: Hey, Louis . . .
VONNE: Prick.
GABE: Hey, Vonne . . .
ROSIE: You think you want Henry's car.
GABE: I'll work it over, get it running, get into it and drive until it falls apart. See where we are then. Take a deep breath and dive right in.
ROSIE: You don't have fifty dollars.
GABE: You don't understand finance.
ROSIE: You don't understand Louis.
GABE: Lost my train of thought.
ROSIE: Your train of thought! You do the talking. You tell the stories.
GABE: I'm not talking to you if you're not talking sense, Rosie. What's wrong with Vonne?
VONNE: Fuck off!
GABE: Misses me. Don't worry, honey. Rosie and I is not significant. Won't change a thing. Vonne and I will climb a lot of steps together.
ROSIE: Your pants are too tight and your hair is too long. There is nothing in your stupid head but you. You want Louis to be one thing. You want me to be one thing.
GABE: I want excitement. There's a lot finer things in the world than Henry Jackson with his hands in his pockets. Than Batoche. Than a prairie fire.
VONNE: You can leave Henry out of your discussions.
GABE: Henry?
VONNE: You can stop making fun of him.
GABE: I love women. Sometimes I get the feeling that's about all you can count on to surprise you. Be just as pure and fine as the fire on the lake.
VONNE: You can fuck off. You and your fine fucking talk about big talkers and white men with turnips for brains.
GABE: Louis not talking to you?
VONNE: He's another one.

GABE: You got Louis all wrong. He'll be back. He and I have plans.
ROSIE: Liar.
GABE: Sure. We're going to Cedar Rapids.
ROSIE: Stop laughing at him.
GABE: Well, we're getting out of here for damn sure. Him and I get along.
ROSIE: Like you and I get along. Like a prairie fire.
GABE: I'm going to talk to Louis.
ROSIE: No you aren't.
VONNE: No more.
GABE: *(To ROSIE)* Who says?
ROSIE: I do.
VONNE: I do.
GABE: *(To ROSIE)* Like to see you stop me.
ROSIE: You'll go through that door over my dead body.
GABE: Have to do better than that.
ROSIE: Try and pass me.

ROSIE kicks, aiming for GABE's groin.

GABE: You stay above the belt, Rosie. Jesus, you don't know where to start.
ROSIE: I do what I like.
GABE: Yippee, Rosie!
ROSIE: If you're going to Cedar Rapids, I'm going with you. Louis driving your fifty dollar car. And you in the back seat with me, keeping quiet.
GABE: Can't help liking you.
VONNE: You're staying off of Louis' back.
ROSIE: *(As their fight continues)* Crazy bastard! You and Louis get along, sure you do. If he is playing your rules. If you win. You got nothing going for you but wild crazy talk and there isn't anyone can understand it. Isn't anyone would care if you did make any sense. I want you out of here! You aren't leaving, Gabe!

ROSIE frantically rushes GABE. VONNE joins in, and the fight continues through the following dialogue.

VONNE: Just one reason he wants to go to Cedar Rapids. Get some quiet drinking done.
GABE: Now just a minute, Vonne.
VONNE: And he can't do that when you're around.
GABE: I'm not fighting the both of you girls.

114

VONNE: You're too young and stupid for him, Gabie. He remembers what that's like. He drinks beer about it. He remembers what it's like and he don't need you to remind him.
GABE: I want to explain to you about the victory at Duck Lake.
VONNE: Suck Duck Lake.
GABE: When Dumont had twenty-five men on horseback and a few men on foot and Crozier had one hundred soldiers, the Prince Albert volunteers, with cannon.
VONNE: You can leave him in peace.
ROSIE: You can stay here. You can go. You can make up your mind.
GABE: See Dumont's brother, Isidore, went out to meet Crozier's men. He was waving a white blanket.
ROSIE: White blankets. Sure.
GABE: And Crozier, rather than thinking that he wanted to parlay, figured Dumont was trying to outflank him.
VONNE: Rather have Louis falling blind drunk . . .
GABE: So he shot Isidore . . .
VONNE: . . . falling blind drunk than have you at the best of times.
GABE: Shot Isidore dead, goddamn it.
VONNE: I got him Rosie.
GABE: Well, the Metis did outflank the government men. The government couldn't do anything right. They racked up their cannon. They loaded the shell in before the powder so they couldn't get the shell out.
ROSIE: I don't have to stay here.
GABE: The Canadians said the Metis fired the first shot. Well, that was a lie.
ROSIE: I don't have to stay here. I don't have to listen to you.
VONNE: We don't.
ROSIE: Crazy bastard!
VONNE: Come on, Rosie.
ROSIE: Crazy bastard!

They exit.

GABE: Crozier claimed heavy casualties on Dumont's side. Eighty men. Well, that was a lie. Maybe there were eight men in the neighbourhood heard the shots. And come to see what was going on. But by the time they got there, the Canadians was long gone. Nothing to see but Louis Riel riding up and down waving a big silver cross.

GABE has had much the worse of his battle with the girls. He is flat out, exhausted. LOUIS enters from the bar.

115

LOUIS: *(Amused)* You all right?

GABE: My hand's bleeding, that's all.

LOUIS: Can you get up?

GABE: I can do anything! Anything! Can't I? My ears are ringing. Look at that. Blood. Amazing, isn't it? Reminds me of the time I locked the keys inside an old car I had. I was drinking then. So I said, "we can fix that" and I put my fist through the window and I got the keys and my hand was bleeding and my arm, like it is now.

LOUIS: You hand's not bleeding.

GABE: It's bloody.

LOUIS: It's your nose.

GABE: It's my head.

LOUIS: Sit down. Take it easy.

GABE: You're all right, aren't you? Not a mark on you. Not much of a fighter, are you?

LOUIS: Got a beer in my hand.

GABE: I'll join you.

LOUIS: First long step to being like me and Norbert. Fucked up traplines, pickled eggs, shuffle board. Draught beer politics at the Empress Hotel.

GABE: I got my own Temperance League.

LOUIS: So I've seen. Got your own code of ethics. Coat of arms. Got your own newspaper. Print your own news. Make every god-damned night at a goddamned half-assed gas station into goddamned opening day at the goddamn Calgary Stampede.

GABE: So Rosie told me.

LOUIS: She's got a way with words.

GABE: Spellbinder.

LOUIS: You've got a good friend in Rosie.

GABE: I appreciate her interest.

LOUIS: Rosie sees where you're going.

GABE: More than I do.

LOUIS: Well, some are better at it.

GABE: It's kind of funny. I tell you I'm moving in with Rosie and I tell her I'm going to Cedar Rapids with you. And what I'm really going to do is stay in Batoche. End up killing some simple-minded white man like Henry Jackson in a bar room fight that gets out of hand.

> *GABE and LOUIS enter Jackson's Service Station where HENRY is sitting around with VONNE and ROSIE.*

HENRY: You know, I always had trouble thinking of things to say to people until I read this magazine with some good advice. Talk about what you know about, it said, and if there's one thing

I know about, it's cars. Well, happens that is something that just about everybody is interested in. Cars. So a good thing to do instead of standing around looking stupid, is to turn to the next fellow. Ask him what kind of car he drives. First time I tried it, the fellow drove a Chevy and he had a lot of trouble with the carburetor.

GABE: I'd like you to sell me that Ford you got out back.
HENRY: Seemed like he'd keep getting dirt in the fuel line.
GABE: Want to buy that Ford, Henry.
HENRY: Oh, I couldn't do that.
GABE: Why not?
HENRY: Well, it isn't worth much, Gabe. No. You wouldn't want to buy it.
LOUIS: He can get it running.
GABE: Hell, Henry. I won't lie to you. I got it running.
HENRY: Ford out back?
GABE: Sure.
HENRY: That's something, isn't it?
GABE: All the nights out here on the highway when I should have been watching you drink yourself stupid.
HENRY: That old Ford.
GABE: Fifty dollars.
HENRY: What do you want with that old Ford?
GABE: Well, the first thing we're going to do is paint it up like a medicine show.
LOUIS: That's because he's hell for style.
GABE: The second thing I'm going to do is take a leaf from your book, Henry . . .
HENRY: Yes?
GABE: Going to wire the whole vehicle for sound.
HENRY: Got a tip for you there.
GABE: There'll be speakers built in the doors. Under the floor boards. Inside the upholstery like a voice in your pillow.
LOUIS: We will broadcast from that car.
GABE: That car is going to be powered by sound, Henry.
HENRY: Needs an FM radio.
GABE: And then I'm going to jump parole and drive.
HENRY: Where are you going?
GABE: Where we going, Louis?
HENRY: Is Louis going?
GABE: We're all going.
HENRY: Who?
GABE: We're all going.
HENRY: Me?
GABE: Where we going, Henry?
HENRY: Well. Me. Well. Don't mind if I do.

GABE: You look to be the kind of man who wants to see the ocean. That's where we'll go, Henry. Stopping only in Cedar Rapids, Iowa, where Louis and I, since we're sure-footed, have a keen sense of balance . . . we'll be working in high steel construction for a while.

HENRY: All of us?

GABE: And Rosie and Vonne are going. Keep that back seat homey. *(The girls are playing cards and GABE includes them in the story)* The girls are going to dress up like gypsies. Tell fortunes. That's how we'll paint the car, Henry. Like a gypsy tea room.

VONNE: Rosie and Vonne heard enough of your bullshit.

ROSIE: We're staying right here.

GABE: Not when you hear about it. Bought the car for you. Have the doors painted yellow. Close to gold. With your name on. Rosie. That's a name. Curling all up over the door, looks like it's alive. And Ee-Vonne. Spell it with a Y.

VONNE: Want to tell Gabic's fortune, Rosie?

LOUIS: Gabe. Will. Make. It. Work. From the antenna on the tower in Batoche, Saskatchewan, Gabe will broadcast on an assigned frequency of sixty thousand kilaherts at a dangerous altitude with a power of millions of watts. As he completes his broadcast day, good-night and good morning.

ROSIE: Gabie is a tall dark stranger. Thinks he came from across the sea somewhere. In a boat. To rescue somebody. Looks like a white man with a Bible in his hand. Standing right in front of the sun with a fierce-looking, stupid-looking smile.

> She pushes the cards she has laid out together and looks up for his reaction.

GABE: Jesus, Rosie.

VONNE: Want to go to the ocean with him?

ROSIE: I want to go to bed with him.

VONNE: I want to go to Regina. Think he'll get that far?

GABE: Take you where you want to go. Seen the error of my ways.

ROSIE: I heard that before.

GABE: Don't get anywhere by fighting you, do I? You're tough, Rosie. Beat me to the floor.

ROSIE: Because I'm sick of stories!

GABE: Ride the river with you. Sure. Vonne, too. Tough little broads.

ROSIE: All in your head. Crazy stories. What you need is an axe.

GABE: I need to fly, Rosie.

ROSIE: I don't care.

GABE: You can fly.

118

ROSIE: Sure I can.
GABE: Come on then.

He picks her up and spins her around.

VONNE: And we'll paint on the front of it. "Gabie's Crazy Ford."
Louis can be President.
LOUIS: Not for long.
VONNE: Sure you can.
LOUIS: I'm tired, Vonne. I'm here for the ride.
VONNE: We'll go to Regina. Sure. Why not?
ROSIE: We'll eat in restaurants and sleep in hotels. Ride around
in big cars, blowing smoke in people's faces.
VONNE: Remember Gabie's mother. She looked like his sister.
We'll be like that.
ROSIE: We'll walk into this Chinese Restaurant, with red carpets
and white napkins and bamboo screens.
GABE: Goddamn right.
ROSIE: And everyone there will be eating something different.
And everyone, when they see us come in, they'll yell. They'll
ask us over to their table. Want to feed us with their fingers. All
the best parts.
VONNE: And it won't be a screwing hotel like the Empress.
Where the sheets get thin. An honest to god, stay overnight hotel.
With suitcases. Okay, Louis?
LOUIS: I'll keep going as long as I last. If I last that long.
GABE: Going to Regina, Louis.
LOUIS: Going to stop for a minute.
VONNE: *(To ROSIE)*   What are you going to wear?
ROSIE: To the restaurant?
VONNE: I'm going to wear whatever I like.
ROSIE: I'm going to wear black. Every day. And a dress with a
train.
GABE: Hey, Louis . . .
LOUIS: Leave me, Gabe. Let me watch.
GABE: Come on, Louis. You'll tell them. Remember. You met
me when I was a punk kid in the Prince Albert Pen. Singing songs
about Gabriel Dumont.

GABE sings and LOUIS claps.

GABE: *(Sings)*
Back at Batoche where we started from
There's times that life gets wearisome
The wind's too cold and the air's too dry
And there's telephone wires across the sky

119

There's nothing to do but drink and fight
And watch the hockey of a Saturday night.

What the white man taught the Metis
Told them virtue was its own reward
Now they're waving at their Saviour
Louis Riel in a fifty dollar Ford.

> *During this, LOUIS and GABE, followed by HENRY,
> leave the gas station for the Empress Hotel's famous
> Tahiti Room. HENRY is puzzled but eager to take
> part in whatever fun is going on.*

HENRY: Something I want to talk to you about.
GABE: We're coming to your part, Henry. Just sit patient.
HENRY: Something we have to discuss.

GABE: *(Sings)*
It might be Henry Jackson's dream
To score for the Toronto team
But me, I'm leaving this hotel
Going to find Dumont and Louis Riel
Dumont shot and Louis scored
Keeps a man from getting bored.

What the white man taught the Metis
Told them virtue was its own reward
Now they're waving at their Saviour
Louis Riel in his fifty dollar Ford.

HENRY: *(Clapping along)* Ha!
GABE: You see the beauty of it, Henry. Because you have always
wanted to see the ocean and Louis always wanted to see Cedar
Rapids. Rosie always wanted to tell fortunes.
HENRY: Can't sell you the car, Gabe.
LOUIS: Doesn't make any difference, Henry . . .
HENRY: Gabe?
LOUIS: It's a joke. It's a story. Gabe is flying. He don't need a car.
HENRY: I can't sell you the car, Gabe.
GABE: *(A little dangerous)* Sure you can.
HENRY: You don't have any money.
GABE: So what?
HENRY: So you can't buy the car.
GABE: Money, Henry? You can take it out in trade.
HENRY: What I mean is . . .
GABE: I thought you could get the supplies together. The
provisions. You got a logical mind.

HENRY: I mean I was talking to Charles.

GABE: Charles ain't coming.

HENRY: The thing is Charles was looking to see a certain amount of improvements . . .

GABE: Charles has got no sense of fun.

HENRY: . . . around the place. He got some whitewash I was going to show you. I told him how busy we been.

GABE: No special talents. No fun. No place for him.

HENRY: Charles figures you're out of a job.

GABE: I see.

HENRY: So I can't sell you the car, Gabe.

GABE: Well, shit.

HENRY: Well, I tried to explain to him . . .

GABE: Well, I wouldn't worry, Henry. Kind of funny when you look at it right. See the joke, Louis?

HENRY: I wouldn't want to spoil your plans.

GABE: Won't change a thing.

HENRY: I wouldn't want to stop the trip.

GABE: Can't depend on you all my life. And your good nature. Have to depend on myself, don't I, Henry?

HENRY: Sure. There's other cars, eh, Gabe?

GABE: Look on the bright side.

HENRY: Sure, that's right.

GABE: Take the good with the bad.

HENRY: Take the bitter with the batter.

GABE: Which ocean do you want to see?

HENRY: Me?

GABE: Cedar Rapids is as close to the middle as makes no difference. Won't matter which way we go after that.

HENRY: Well, the thing is, like I said about the car. What Charles said . . .

GABE: Going swimming.

HENRY: I can't swim, Gabe.

GABE: I'll teach you.

HENRY: You don't have to do that . . .

GABE: I'm glad to do it, Henry. Friendship.

HENRY laughs, uncomfortably.

HENRY: The reason I like drinking with you is you're both hellish fine fellows. Hard drinkers. Good company. I like you. There's only one trouble with you, that's you're not responsible. I mean Gabe here, Louis, because you got a head on your shoulders. But Gabie, you never know that he isn't going to take off some place just because he feels like it. Now, I can understand that in a young fellow. Feel like taking off myself sometimes. But you can't run a gas station that way. No sir.

121

GABE: Your brother's gas station isn't really running, Henry. It's just sitting there, looking kind of sad.
HENRY: Could make something out of that place. Good location.
GABE: Yeah, it's peaceful. Don't get a lot of traffic.
HENRY: If I had help I could depend on.
GABE: Buy me a drink, Henry.
LOUIS: You don't want to do that.
HENRY: Gabe goes crazy when he's drinking.
GABE: I'm going to get drunk, really drunk. I'm going to beat him unconscious. I'm going to steal his fucking car.
HENRY: I'm trying to talk sense to you, Gabie.
GABE: I'm going to let Henry buy the first round.
HENRY: You tell him, Louis. How he's acting foolish.
LOUIS: You're acting foolish, Gabe.
GABE: Oh yeah?
LOUIS: You're sitting around drinking with a broken down rodeo rider and a half-wit.
GABE: Nice talk.
HENRY: Who are you calling a half-wit?
GABE: Who's the broken down rodeo rider, more to the point?
HENRY: Who are you calling a half-wit?
GABE: I got no quarrel with you, Louis.
LOUIS: Why not?
GABE: Get me my own big yellow car some day. Drive it through the biggest towns in Saskatchewan. Sure. Making speeches from the back seat. Have people falling back in amazement, never having heard speaking like it before. It'll all be true, see. No word of a lie. Talking Metis rights. Singing Metis rights. Get a little fiddle breakdown, we'll have everyone back on their feet. Dancing on behind me.
HENRY: Who's calling who a half-wit?
LOUIS: It's me calling you. You can take it as a compliment.
HENRY: I take exception.
GABE: Shut up, Henry.
HENRY: No man's going to say that to me.
GABE: We always say it, Henry. You keep coming back for more. You like the attention.
HENRY: No drunken lazy, no good dirty Indian's going to say it, that's for damn sure.
GABE: Leave him, Louis. He's a sick little bastard.

LOUIS has HENRY and he's beating him brutally.
GABE tries to separate them.

GABE: Leave him go, Louis, goddamn it. You'll kill him. He's drunk, that's all. Rest of the week he follows you around like a dog. Goddamn it, you'll kill him. I don't understand you.

LOUIS has beaten HENRY very badly. He stretches back for one last punch or kick, wonders why he is bothering and drops HENRY to the ground. He takes HENRY's cigarettes out of his pocket and lights one. GABE watches him. HENRY pulls himself together and out of the bar.

HENRY: Goddamn fucking Louis Riel cowboy movie.

GABE: You're goddamn crazy, Louis. Don't let him bother you. Jesus, I would have beat him if I thought you wanted it done. He knows me.

LOUIS: He's worthless.

GABE: Sure he is. And that's why he's here, goddamn it. Why he wants to be like me. Just like me. Like you. And that's why he's going crawling home to Charles right now and Charles is going to send you back to jail so fast . . .

HENRY: *(As he leaves)* You know what they did to Louis Riel. They hanged the son of a bitch.

GABE: What are you doing, Louis?

LOUIS: I'm going to go to jail.

GABE: You go to jail, it's your own fucking fault.

LOUIS: I'm going to jail and you're not.

GABE: You're crazy, Louis.

LOUIS: I see Gabriel Dumont. He is afflicted and ashamed. He does not look at me. He looks to his future. His present. He is an outlaw. He has nothing and he blames me for it.

GABE: Okay. Sure. We'll go. We'll steal a car and drive. You want to? I've done it before.

LOUIS: The Canadians must punish before they can forgive. I will allow them to punish me again.

GABE: That's shit. That's Riel talking again.

LOUIS: Riel said: "There will be a trial. I will speak there. I will use it as a platform to talk of Metis rights. The Canadians will listen. There will be an investigation in Parliament. All the grievances, my people's grievances, will be exposed. I will fulfill my mission. I will speak . . ."

LOUIS exits as VONNE enters with ROSIE. VONNE is very angry.

VONNE: I hate Henry for being so stupid. I hate Henry's goddamn big brother Charles. I hate Louis for wasting his time with either of them. Louis beats Henry up. Louis goes back to jail, so what good does that do? You're always beating Henry up.

GABE: But he doesn't take me serious.

VONNE: And Louis goes to jail for it.

123

GABE: Parole.

VONNE: Parole.

GABE: Parole violation.

VONNE: Is that all you can say, parole violation? Because what is Louis supposed to do? Let Henry hire him and fire him and call him dirt. He's supposed to let you beat Henry up because you're not serious about it. You beating Henry, that doesn't count. Keeps things lively. No one holds a grudge about it. No one holds a goddamn grudge and Henry's little brain just goes on rattling around in Henry's big thick head while Louis bangs his head against a wall. Parole violation. Parole violation. Parole violation.

GABE: I don't know what to say, Vonne. Is that all right?

ROSIE: Talk to Henry for her.

GABE: Oh, Rosie, honey . . .

ROSIE: Charles put him up to it.

GABE: So what?

ROSIE: Henry doesn't know anything.

GABE: Poor old Henry.

ROSIE: Do it.

GABE: What if I beat him up again? I could kill him.

ROSIE: You won't.

GABE: How do you know?

ROSIE: It will all strike you funny. At the last minute. You'll be laughing too hard.

GABE: I'd like to go out in the bush again. For a while. No, really. Because I love it. Because the Welfare Department doesn't take me serious, that's for damn sure. And I could get Norbert's traps together. Christ, that would be a Christian act of mercy.

ROSIE: Shut up, Gabe.

GABE: I'm just telling you.

ROSIE: You're making excuses.

GABE: I got no excuse, Rosie. I love the bush and I can't take Jackson's Gas Station serious. I think it looks stupid out there on the highway all by itself. When I'm working there . . . when I'm working for Charles, I feel like a rodeo clown . . .

ROSIE: Well, you aren't . . .

GABE: Shit, I'm a half-breed pump jockey. I'm a disaster. I'm better in the bush. Shit, Rosie, every time I come out of the bush and I'm still together, Charles and Henry, they see they're the clowns.

ROSIE: Charles and Henry never think about the bush.

GABE: I'm a comic book hero, Rosie.

ROSIE: I guess so.

GABE: You don't want to go. Do you? You don't like the bush.

ROSIE: I don't like mosquitoes. I like it in the fall.

GABE: Little white lies.

124

ROSIE: You could be an outlaw. In the woods. Nobody would see you again. Ever. Just tell stories about you.
GABE: You see too many movies.
ROSIE: Why not?
GABE: You could go to Regina. You and Vonne. Every night they'd turn the gas-light on. The big glass chandelier. And you'd come in, down the stairs, eating a flower. Everybody standing around the bottom of the stairs, clapping their fists together.
ROSIE: I don't know. I don't think so.
GABE: You got very romantic ideas.
ROSIE: Will you talk to Henry?
GABE: Jesus, Rosie, I said I would.

HENRY enters as ROSIE exits. GABE watches him. Nothing is going on, although when he notices GABE, HENRY pretends to be busy.

HENRY: What are you doing here?
GABE: Come to say good-bye to you.
HENRY: That's a stupid thing to do.
GABE: Because Louis beat you when I should have done it? Come on Henry, I don't hold a grudge.
HENRY: The thing about you is you got no sense of responsibility. You or Louis. None of you.
GABE: I'm going off in the woods, Henry.
HENRY: You aren't going anywhere. You're on parole. Like Louis was.
GABE: Going to see how long I last. On my own. No supplies. No pack. No gun.
HENRY.   Parole. That's a responsibility. That's an obligation. Parole. That's a promise. You wouldn't give that a second thought. None of you.
GABE: Us half-breeds are very wily in the woods.
HENRY: You half-breeds aren't responsible.
GABE: We're very close to nature.
HENRY: You drink too much.
GABE: When I was a kid, I ran away from the correctional institute. I lived off the land till the break-up. Only year I never got in trouble. Not till spring. Then they finally got it together, came and got me.
HENRY: Last winter. Over at the Empress. Two half-breeds, a woman and a man, Charles told me. Over there spending their welfare cheques. They left their kids out in their broken down old car with the heat off. The kids fell asleep. Those two were so drunk they drove all the way home, forgot about the kids, left them in the car all night. They froze to death, the kids. That's half-breeds drinking for you. Or maybe they were Indians.

125

GABE: Even if you knew anything about hunting, fishing, trapping, anything about the land and how to use it, you'd be dead in the bush,. Henry. You're a city man, Henry. You can't live by yourself.
HENRY: Even if you didn't drink, you'd still have no sense of responsibility.
GABE: You win, Henry.
HENRY: I'm not afraid of you. Or crazy Louis.
GABE: Who?
HENRY: Crazy Louis.
GABE: Louis wasn't crazy.
HENRY: Sure he was.
GABE: I wouldn't say that.
HENRY: Well, it's true. Beat me up and where did it get him? Back in the Prince Albert Pen. Sure. Good place for him. Bang his head against the bars crazy. Ha.
GABE: Nothing crazy about beating you. Wouldn't want you to think that.
HENRY: You'd never get away with it.
GABE: I wouldn't beat you, Henry.
HENRY: No.
GABE: All of us half-breeds are very sociable.
HENRY: Yeah.
GABE: True?
HENRY: Hell, I know that.
GABE: Sure. We know how to have a party.
HENRY: Well, you're right there.
GABE: Friendly. Give you the shirt off my back. You want it?
HENRY: Well, I got a shirt like it.
GABE: And I don't have to beat you, Henry. Because all of us half-breeds, we're hunters. We got special knowledge. Of the future. When my hand moves like this, that means something's going to happen. Or when there's a twitch in my neck. Here.
HENRY: Like the time you told me that the spring flooding was going to knock the bridge out and I told Charles and he didn't believe me. So he drove into town and stranded himself. Had to stay overnight.
GABE: That's right.
HENRY: Wonderful thing.
GABE: Sure. I can see things you can't see. Like Louis Riel. Riding out of Montana. Saw a tree on the hill. And he said to Dumont. That's a tree, isn't it? I thought it was a gallows. With me hanging from it.
HENRY: You and Louis Riel. I heard that before.
GABE: I can see you beaten.
HENRY: What?

126

GABE: It's a vision. I can see you lying there on the floor, looking like something out of one of those comic books. Not the ones with the people. The animal books. Where the stupid looking cat gets rolled out and hung up to dry.
HENRY: Rolled out?
GABE: Lying there, Henry. Looking stupid.
HENRY: Where?
GABE: I guess someone's finally done it right. Someone's finally kicked your teeth down your throat.
HENRY: You?
GABE: Not me. You got to understand I'm not threatening you, Henry. I think it's comical. I think it's kind of sad in a way.
HENRY: I don't know what you're talking about.
GABE: Because you're stupid, Henry. Because you're not afraid of me. Or Louis. Because you think we're crazy. You don't have the brains of a rabbit, Henry.

GABE walks off into a spectacular prairie sunset.
Fade to black.

RED EMMA

Queen of the Anarchists

To M.K.
The finest mind in Canadian Theatre

Act One

*In the original production, a two-level set made it
possible to switch quickly from scene to scene.
There was a table on the lower level which was
used for Sach's Cafe, the* Freiheit *office and the
anarchists' commune. On the upper level there was
a speaker's podium.*

Sach's Cafe. 1890.

HELEN: *(Sings)*
I was young at Sach's Cafe
I drank my coffee black
You could find me talking politics
At a table in the back
All my friends were beautiful
All the talk was good
The rooms were always smoky
And I never understood
Half the things I found I said
Half the thoughts inside my head
Half the books I said I read
Why the coffee tasted sweet

This is the song of Sach's Cafe
This is the song of years I've lost
This is the song of happy times
This is the song of the holocaust

I was young at Sach's Cafe
The coffee tasted sweet
You could find me talking politics
I never had to eat
All my friends were crazy drunk
All their lies were true
The answers seemed so easy
The things I had to do
How my work would be begun
How I had to race the sun
How the well-known west was won
Why I couldn't speak.

131

*Sach's Cafe is attended by PARKS, a Pinkerton
man disguised as a waiter. EMMA and HELEN are
sitting together over a glass of tea. HELEN is
hoping to pick up some boys. BERKMAN and
FEDYA enter. FEDYA sits at the far end of their
table. BERKMAN paces.*

BERKMAN: I want two steaks and two coffees . . . Make that
a pot of coffee and a three pound steak! Fried potatoes. String
beans. Lots of butter on the beans.
EMMA: Who is he?
HELEN: Alexander Berkman.
EMMA: You know the one I mean?
HELEN: His friend is an artist. Fedya. They call them the
"twins" because they are always together.
EMMA: Berkman is the tall one.
HELEN: Hello, Fedya.
BERKMAN: I want sliced tomato on the side. And dill pickle.
EMMA: Does Alexander Berkman always jump around like
that?
BERKMAN: *(To the waiter)* I want all of that, comrade. As
soon as you can.
HELEN: He eats more than anyone else. He drinks more than
anyone else. He jumps around more than anyone else.
EMMA: And he's going to eat standing up?
HELEN: I don't know, Emma.
EMMA: It makes me nervous watching him.
HELEN: You don't look nervous.
BERKMAN: You are Emma Goldman.

*HELEN slides over to FEDYA's end of the table
leaving EMMA a clear field. EMMA doesn't notice.
She is watching BERKMAN.*

HELEN: Hello, Fedya.
BERKMAN: You are Emma Goldman. You just came to New
York. The only man in New York you knew was Solatoroff and
you went to his address but Solatoroff moves twice a week and
all the janitor knew was he'd gone to Montgomery Street. And
you, Emma Goldman, went to every house on Montgomery
Street until you found him. You found Solatoroff. You found
Sach's Cafe. You found one of the famous Minkin sisters. Which
one? Is it Helen?
HELEN: Yes.
BERKMAN: And now you find Alexander Berkman. An
extravagant spirit to match your extravagant eyes.

132

EMMA: How old are you?
BERKMAN: I'm eighteen. *(He lights a match and holds it up to her face)* You are all of nineteen and I want to watch you closely.

EMMA blows out the match.

EMMA: Children burn themselves so easily.
BERKMAN: I'm a revolutionary. I love fire. Your comrade Solatoroff will tell you that.
FEDYA: He wouldn't let you near her.
BERKMAN: Emma is not bound to Solatoroff.
EMMA: Emma is not bound to any man.

There is a pause. EMMA and BERKMAN are delighted with each other. EMMA chuckles. BERKMAN chuckles. HELEN is pleased things are going so well.

HELEN: Shall we have another glass of tea, Emma?
BERKMAN: I am making a speech this evening. About revolution. You will come and hear me.
HELEN: We are going to hear Solatoroff.
FEDYA: He teaches anarchy to night school classes.
BERKMAN: You will hear me instead. Take the Minkin sister if you will. Come on.
HELEN: What is Sasha's topic, Fedya?
BERKMAN: I will speak on propaganda of the deed, I think.
FEDYA: You will introduce the main speaker.
BERKMAN: Johann Most is not the main speaker, Fedya . . .

Pronounce MOST to rhyme with cost, *not strictly correct but less confusing in English.*

EMMA: Johann Most? Tonight?
BERKMAN: . . . We are all equals. We are comrades in anarchy.
FEDYA: Tell Most he's equal. If you can get him off the grandstand.
EMMA: I came to New York to hear Johann Most.
BERKMAN: You will hear me as well.
EMMA: Because in Rochester, I read his newspaper. He is revolution.
BERKMAN: Most will send me to Rochester this month. On a speaking tour.
EMMA: Do you know him very well?
BERKMAN: Of course I do.

EMMA: I read everything he says.
FEDYA: You are a victim of publicity.
EMMA: I know him.
FEDYA: *(Flamboyantly)* A long black coat, a big black hat, a big black bomb. They draw him in cartoons in Rochester. They call him the devil and make him the symbol of anarchy.
EMMA: He is the lifeblood of anarchy.
BERKMAN: You are nineteen. You are very impressionable.
EMMA: I am twenty.

He pulls her to her feet.

BERKMAN: Come with me. Are you coming?
EMMA: I'm older than you are.
BERKMAN: You have a lot to teach me I suppose.
EMMA: You have a lot to learn.
HELEN: Are you going to hear Johann Most, Fedya?
FEDYA: Yes, there's a free lunch.

They exit. PARKS enters to clear the table and follow them out with the bill. HENRY CLAY FRICK enters, on the upper level, followed by KREIDERMAN, who has a portfolio of correspondence.

KREIDERMAN: You speak to the Unity Club at ten, Mr. Frick. I have given the press copies of the text of your remarks. You lunch with Mr. Andrew Carnegie and he will want these figures. These letters are requests for proxies in the matter of the stock options. These letters are answers to requests for funds, solicitations, letters of sympathy and condolence . . .

PARKS enters bustling. He is carrying a newspaper which he hands to KREIDERMAN officiously.

PARKS: There is a cartoon. On the editorial page. Mr. Frick is shown grinding the faces of the poor in the mud.
KREIDERMAN: Mr. Frick doesn't want to see that kind of trash, Mr. Parks.
FRICK: Find out who owns that newspaper and buy it.

FRICK exits.

KREIDERMAN: You heard Mr. Frick, Mr. Parks. Who owns that newspaper?

PARKS: It's a German newspaper, sir. From New York. How do you say "owner" in German?

> *KREIDERMAN and PARKS exit. BERKMAN enters and mounts the podium to introduce JOHANN MOST. He is carrying the banner of anarchy — a red flag is more exciting than the correct black. During his speech EMMA, HELEN and FEDYA enter on the lower level, also with flags.*

BERKMAN: Johann Most began his work as a revolutionary pamphleteer and a member of the Reichstag. He was persecuted for his opinions. He was exiled from his native Germany. In England he was imprisoned because he supported the assassination of Alexander II. His newspaper *Freiheit* was suppressed. Johann Most, brave spirit, now a free voice in America. I am proud to introduce him.

> *MOST enters, pausing only briefly to shake BERKMAN's hand and show BERKMAN is his protégé. He is an electric speaker.*

MOST: We will see the world change. We are dedicated and determined men. We are men who know that a bloodless revolution is no revolution at all. We are men who understand the power of the individual act of violence. The Attentat! We can tear out the throat of tyranny.

We will change the world. That is why we act. If our violence brings our death then we will be anarchy's martyrs.

Anarchy has martyrs now.

In 1886, all across the country, workers demanded the eight-hour day. In Chicago, at the McCormick Harvester Company, a workers' meeting was attacked by police. Men and women were beaten. Several were killed. To protest the outrage, the workers met in Haymarket Square. A quiet, orderly meeting. Carter Harrison, the mayor of Chicago, said that. A quiet, orderly meeting. It was clouding over. A light rain began. Very few remained to hear the last speakers. The police attacked again.

> *EMMA's following interjections into MOST's text should be like a litany. We should get the impression that she feels this story deeply and that MOST becomes aware of her presence at the meeting because of the depth of her feeling.*

EMMA: Captain Ward, accompanied by a strong force of police, suddenly appeared on the square. The police fell upon the people, clubbing them unmercifully . . .

MOST: There was a bomb. A bomb was thrown, killing a number of police officers and wounding many others. No one knew who threw the bomb but orders were immediately issued for the arrest of every prominent anarchist in Chicago.

EMMA: The bourgeois of Chicago asked for blood . . .

MOST: The police began a campaign of terror which ended when five men were sentenced to die by hanging . . .

EMMA: Albert Parsons, August Spies, Louis Lingg . . .

MOST: Five men innocent of crime and in no way connected with it . . .

EMMA: Adolph Fischer . . . George Engel . . .

MOST: Five martyrs. Albert Parsons. August Spies. Louis Lingg. Adolph Fischer. George Engel.

EMMA: August Spies knew he was a martyr. He knew that ordinary people could see farther than vicious attacks in the press. Ordinary men and women were not as blind as the justice in American courts. August Spies answered his death sentence in these words: "Our silence will speak louder than the voices that you strangle today." The eleventh of November. A five mile line of workers followed the martyrs to their graves.

All sing, waving banners.

November Eleven
The Haymarket Martyrs
Were strangled and silenced
But we can be free
Their voices were ringing
In moments of silence
The martyrs are singing to me

Five men dead
They've made us strong
Fifty thousand sing their song

November Eleven
Means we have our martyrs
Their voices are ringing
And we can be free
The silence is singing
The martyrs speak wonders
The voices mean freedom to me.

At the end of the song MOST approaches EMMA.
BERKMAN is trying to get her attention but
EMMA's concentration is totally on MOST.

MOST: Do you speak English?
EMMA: Me?
MOST: I'll lend you some books. Not English. You read
German?
EMMA: Yes, I do.
MOST: You want to learn about anarchy.
EMMA: More than anything. Of course I do.
MOST: *(Gently mocking)*   More than anything. Of course I do.
EMMA: It's my first day in New York. I came to New York to
hear you speak.
MOST: I am enchanted by your enthusiasm.
EMMA: About the Haymarket Martyrs. It was those events. In
Chicago. They awakened my political conscience.
MOST: *(Amused)*   Really?
EMMA: Yes.
MOST: I'm sorry. I don't mean to be patronizing.
EMMA: Oh, you aren't.
MOST: No?
EMMA: I came to New York to meet you.
MOST: We'll drink to that. Shall we? We will go to Sach's
Cafe. We will order Liebfraumilch.
BERKMAN: Emma . . .
EMMA: Here is your comrade Alexander Berkman.
MOST: Berkman is zealous, dedicated. We have work for him
to do.
EMMA: He said you will send him to Rochester. To speak.
That's where I'm from.
MOST: Give the girl her shawl, Berkman, and drop her hand, if
you permit?

MOST and EMMA exit.

HELEN: As Johann Most tells us, man does not need authority,
law or government to keep him virtuous.
FEDYA: *(To BERKMAN)*   Did you ask about the tour?
BERKMAN: No.
HELEN: I find his remarks instructive and illuminating. And
uplifting. He is a man of extraordinary vision, is he not?
FEDYA: If Anna Minkin sees Most's vision then it must be
large and clear.
HELEN: I'm Helen. As you know.

137

FEDYA: Anna is the one who follows Sasha around. You're the one who follows me.
HELEN: He isn't serious. Is he, Sasha?
BERKMAN: Fedya is never serious. Most is always serious. What is your friend Emma like?

Exit BERKMAN, FEDYA, HELEN. KREIDERMAN enters, disguised as a drunk, to establish Sach's Cafe. MOST and EMMA enter.

MOST: Liebfraumilch!

PARKS appears with a bottle.

EMMA: I've never tasted wine before.
MOST: *(Amused)* I'm sure you haven't.
EMMA: Except the kind my mother made for Passover.
MOST: Your name is Emma, isn't it?
EMMA: Yes it is.
MOST: And you are from Rochester?
EMMA: Yes.
MOST: You will promise not to tell me about your mother's wine, Emma.
EMMA: I don't want to bore you. I don't want to talk about myself. I want to learn about anarchy.
MOST: Prosit, my young naive lady.
EMMA: I've read everything you ever wrote. *(MOST drains his glass and pours another)* Everything they printed in Rochester, I mean. *(MOST drains his glass and pours another)* Do you acknowledge the thought of William Godwin at all?
MOST: Another bottle please.

He pours himself another drink and takes a deep breath. He finds EMMA's intensity overpowering. Both EMMA and MOST drink a lot in this scene. By its end, they are drunk.

EMMA: Because you say "a bloodless revolution is no revolution at all." Which is what Godwin says, although of course he is not lead to your conclusion.
MOST: What is needed here is to lighten the atmosphere some-how. Perhaps if I ordered still another bottle of wine and spilled it all over the front of my shirt.
EMMA: I don't understand.
MOST: You are Russian?
EMMA: Yes.

MOST: Perhaps if I threw the wine glasses against the wall.
Drink up. We'll try it.
EMMA: Drink up?
MOST: Toss it back. Like this.
EMMA: Like this?

> *EMMA tries to throw the glass against the wall but
> MOST catches her wrist.*

MOST: You are very charming, my dear. Please excuse the
clumsy compliment.
EMMA: You were talking about anarchy. I didn't want to
interrupt.
MOST: Anarchy. Of course. Anarchy.
EMMA: Yes.
MOST: You want to learn about anarchy?
EMMA: Yes.
MOST: Well, I'm the one to teach you, am I not?
EMMA: As I said.
MOST: I am the master anarchist. Known in Rochester.
EMMA: Yes, you are.
MOST: The path of anarchism is steep and painful. Do you
believe that? Do you have a sense of humour, my very young
lady? You will need it as an anarchist. Steep and painful. Many
have attempted to climb it and fallen back. The price is exacting.
Few men will pay it, few women can pay it . . .
EMMA: There are women here in New York . . .
MOST: Stupid women.
EMMA: Women who work for anarchism . . .
MOST: I don't believe women have revolutionary zeal. Do you?
EMMA: Of course I do.
MOST: Your friend Helen Minkin is looking for a husband.
EMMA: Now you're joking. Now you're patronizing . . .
MOST: Of course she is. She's a young girl. She goes to
meetings only to find out who will take her home from meet-
ings. Stupid.
EMMA: Helen Minkin is my comrade.
MOST: You hunt together?
EMMA: I do not hunt.
MOST: No, of course not. You dedicate your life to the cause.
EMMA: I do. Yes.
MOST: To anarchy.
EMMA: I do. Yes.
MOST: Parsons. Spies. Lingg. Fischer. Engel. They are the men
you walk with?
EMMA: They are my martyrs.

MOST: Emma speaks ardently.
EMMA: Now you're laughing at me.
MOST: I have need of ardent friendship.

Pause.

EMMA: No you don't. Not me.
MOST: Of course, you.
EMMA: You're joking.
MOST: Why would I joke?
EMMA: I know thousands of people read everything you write. They follow you from one meeting to another just to hear you speak . . .
MOST: Perhaps you will be my student. You can speak ardently. I can teach you to speak well.
EMMA: You mean to speak in public?
MOST: You say you must work for the cause.
EMMA: I'm very nervous. I wouldn't know what to say.
MOST: I can tell you what to say.
EMMA: You're joking, aren't you?
MOST: No.
EMMA: You want me to speak about the cause . . . as Alexander Berkman does . . .
MOST: You will listen to me.
EMMA: . . . I amuse you.
MOST: You make me happy. That's all. Are you drunk?
EMMA: Now you're laughing at me. Are you drunk?
MOST: I'm very serious. I'm happy. You make it possible for me to make plans. Drink up.
EMMA: *(Drinking her glass)* Like this?
MOST: Where will we go now?
EMMA: Everywhere. All over New York.
MOST: This is my first happy evening in a long while.
EMMA: Because I came to New York with hope that I could hear you speak. And we've met so soon. We drink wine together.
MOST: Do you hear me, Emma? It is the first time in years I have been happy.

They exit. KREIDERMAN and PARKS compare notes.

PARKS: Did you hear what they said?
KREIDERMAN: No, I didn't. They were speaking Russian.
PARKS: Is Liebfraumilch a Russian word?

140

KREIDERMAN and PARKS clear the table and exit. BERKMAN and FEDYA enter on the upper level. By the time they reach the lower level it is the Freiheit *office.*

BERKMAN: Labourers arise! The bosses have you in chains. Do you like that, Fedya?
FEDYA: It sounds familiar.
BERKMAN: It's the English translation of my new essay. Here. Look. Fifty copies.
FEDYA: It sounds like your last essay.
BERKMAN: My last essay was about Nihilism and the Attentat.
FEDYA: Labourers arise! The bosses have you in chains. I've heard it before.
BERKMAN: The first statement was something of a personal reminiscence. I recalled my Nihilist uncle Maxim hanged by the Cossacks. This is more of a political diatribe.
FEDYA: Maybe you should find a new translator.
BERKMAN: You don't like it? "Labourers arise!" Perhaps "Workers arise!" Is that correct in English?
EMMA: *(Enters)* Workers arise! That's very stirring.
FEDYA: At least Emma hasn't heard it.
BERKMAN: If you help me mail my broadsheet, Emma, I'll show you New York. I'll take you to the Battery.
EMMA: I've been to the Battery.
BERKMAN: You have?
EMMA: Johann Most took me. To escape the heat.
BERKMAN: Staten Island then.
EMMA: I've been there.
BERKMAN: With Most.
EMMA: Yes.
BERKMAN: Where else have you been? With Most?
EMMA: To Sach's.
BERKMAN: Most has no right to squander money. To go to expensive restaurants . . .
EMMA: It was Sach's . . .
BERKMAN: To drink expensive wines. He is spending money contributed for the movement. He is accountable. I'll tell him myself.

He starts to exit. EMMA stops him.

EMMA: No you won't.
BERKMAN: You are very young in the movement. You know nothing about revolutionary ethics. You can't tell revolutionary right from revolutionary wrong.

141

EMMA: And you can?
BERKMAN: Of course I can.
EMMA: You are eighteen years old, Alexander Berkman . . .
BERKMAN: Experience doesn't make an anarchist. Commit-
ment makes an anarchist. You tell that to Johann Most. No. I'll
tell him myself.
EMMA: No you won't.
BERKMAN: He'll see his error. He'll thank me for it.
EMMA: I will not have Most hurt.
BERKMAN: I will educate him.

> *FEDYA is busy destroying BERKMAN's pamphlets*
> *by folding them into different shapes.*

FEDYA: Ha.
EMMA: We are having a private conversation, Fedya.
BERKMAN: No we aren't.
EMMA: I am.
FEDYA: What is her concern for Most?
EMMA: I am having a private conversation.
BERKMAN: *(Ignoring her)* He is her teacher. He is the King of
the Anarchists.
EMMA: You treat women very badly, don't you? A woman is
never your comrade. A woman is always your child.
FEDYA: Does she see a lot of Most?
EMMA: And if I do, I'm wrong, I suppose?
BERKMAN: At the offices of *Freiheit*. Then at Sach's . . .
FEDYA: With Most.
BERKMAN: Of course with Most.
FEDYA: Practicing anarchy.
BERKMAN: Disguising themselves with false black beards.
FEDYA: Rehearsing the lurk and the skulk.
BERKMAN: Emma wishes to appear in an anarchist cartoon.
FEDYA: Most alone and only Most.
EMMA: I find him remarkable.
FEDYA: He's remarkably fond of taking young girls to the
Freiheit office. He lends them books.
EMMA: Get out of here, Fedya.
BERKMAN: Emma is not interested in Most as a man.
FEDYA: You hope.

> *BERKMAN is too young to want his obvious feeling*
> *for EMMA broadcast publicly. He is annoyed.*

BERKMAN: Fedya is not a good anarchist. He isn't serious
enough. He is a bourgeois.

FEDYA: I'm an artist.
BERKMAN: You are not a worker.
FEDYA: I am a drone. You are a worker and I am a drone.
Buzz, buzz . . .

He begins to tear up a broadsheet.

BERKMAN: You annoy me, Fedya.
FEDYA: That's too bad.
BERKMAN: Anarchy is our only concern. The Cause.
FEDYA: You bore me, Sasha.
BERKMAN: Anarchy is our only concern. The Cause. Isn't that
so, Emma?
EMMA: You're joking.
BERKMAN: I sound like I'm joking. Because I'm cheerful. I
have never been so serious. Emma loves anarchy. As I do.
EMMA: I love other things.
BERKMAN: I don't.
EMMA: Of course you do.
BERKMAN: I don't.
EMMA: You must.
BERKMAN: Why?
EMMA: You must love flowers or going to the theatre or
music or dancing.
BERKMAN: I don't.
EMMA: You love to eat.
BERKMAN: No.
EMMA: You do, Sasha. You eat like a horse.
BERKMAN: You think you have me? You think you've found
me in a contradiction. No. Because I eat ravenously but I never
notice what I eat. I could eat anything. And I must eat some-
thing . . .
FEDYA: You eat a lot, Sasha.
BERKMAN: I eat a lot because I care so much. About anarchy.
FEDYA: I go to the theatre a lot because I care so much.
About anarchy.
BERKMAN: Fedya is something of a fake.
FEDYA: Because I don't talk politics? Emma is tired of
politics.
BERKMAN: Emma? Tired? Talking?
FEDYA: Look Emma. I have a present for you.
EMMA: What is it, Fedya?

*It is whatever fantastic device FEDYA can fashion
from SASHA's broadsheet, e.g. a cocked hat, a
palm tree.*

BERKMAN: It is my essay. My latest essay . . .
EMMA: It's very beautiful . . .
BERKMAN: It is destruction of serious thought. It is useless frivolity.
FEDYA: Feeding Emma's spirit isn't frivolous.
BERKMAN: You are wasteful, Fedya.
FEDYA: You like it, don't you, Emma?
EMMA: Yes, of course I do.
BERKMAN: You're an incurable bourgeois. You're a mindless parasite, Fedya.
FEDYA: No.
BERKMAN: Emma doesn't want it.
FEDYA: Yes she does.
BERKMAN: Of course she doesn't.
FEDYA: You don't know Emma. You know nothing about her.
BERKMAN: What I know about Emma has nothing to do with your wastefulness. Materials. Time. Money. It isn't even your money. You take money from your parents.
FEDYA: And they are revisionist, reactionary, middle-class . . .
BERKMAN: That's right. Yes.
FEDYA: I give you the money. Don't I? I give it all to you.
BERKMAN: And I spend it on anarchy, don't I? Every cent. What's wrong with that?
FEDYA: You are single-minded.
BERKMAN: Of course I am. I'm proud of it.
FEDYA: You are narrow.
BERKMAN: Yes! Yes! I am!
FEDYA: Love everything Emma.
BERKMAN: Don't listen to him, Emma.
FEDYA: Love anarchy and everything else.
BERKMAN: You can't escape. There is no escape from the revolution.
EMMA: *(Exploding)* Boom.
FEDYA: *(For fun)* Boom! Boom!
BERKMAN: *(Annoyed, exploding)* Boom! Boom! Boom!

> *The anarchist kids bounce around booming out each other. FRICK enters, followed by KREIDER-MAN and PARKS. FRICK is instructing his men how to get ahead.*

FRICK: America is the land of opportunity, if you can see the opportunity. Take your irons from the fire. Strike your iron while it's hot. Do you know what I'm talking about, Kreiderman?
KREIDERMAN: Yes, sir.

PARKS: I'd like to talk about this strike, sir. At the Homestead Steel Mills.
KREIDERMAN: It isn't a strike, Mr. Parks. It's a walkout.
FRICK: You feel some sympathy for the men at Homestead?
PARKS: They don't make much money, sir.
KREIDERMAN: Ho. Ho. He's only joking, Mr. Frick.
FRICK: Some men have. Some men have not. But the haves have a responsibility. The haves help the have nots. That is social justice.

> *Exit FRICK.*

PARKS: He makes it sound easy, doesn't he Kreiderman?
KREIDERMAN: Because he's a great man, Mr. Parks.

> *Exit KREIDERMAN and PARKS. Enter EMMA, followed by HELEN. They are in the* Freiheit *office.*

EMMA: I was standing at the gates to the Triangle Factory, shaking this collection box. Listen, Helen, if you worked for the Triangle wouldn't that sound cheer you up? Even if you couldn't afford a penny to drop in the slot? Wouldn't you feel better knowing all these pennies were going to the cause?
HELEN: You love Johann Most?
EMMA: He loves me, Helen. I idolize him.
HELEN: And Sasha?
EMMA: Of course I love Sasha.
HELEN: And Fedya?
EMMA: Yes, I told you. Yes, Fedya, too.
HELEN: Fedya isn't anything like Sasha and Sasha isn't anything like Johann Most.
EMMA: I cannot get the lid off this cash box.
HELEN: That must be why you can love them. All. Both intensely and sincerely.
EMMA: Intensely, yes. Sincerely, yes. Will you open this?
HELEN: All at the same time.
EMMA: You analyze too much, Helen. Your approach is too intellectual.
HELEN: The subject interests me.
EMMA: I'm counting, Helen. I can't talk.
HELEN: If we went down to Sach's right now. And if you met someone as different from those three as they are from each other . . .
EMMA: I don't want to go to Sach's.
HELEN: But if you did. I'm curious. That would make four. Why not four?

EMMA: I feel restless.

HELEN: Let's go to Sach's.

EMMA: I feel homeless.

HELEN: Why not five? Why not six? Why not seven?

EMMA: We'll move in together. We'll be comrades. Fedya. Sasha. Helen. Emma.

HELEN: You're changing the subject, Emma.

EMMA: You sound like my aunt and uncle. When I came to New York from Rochester, I arrived at their gallery, they have a photographic gallery and they said I must stay with them, they must give me their spare room. "Where else would you go, a young woman alone in New York?" . . . Well, of course I had to get away. I went to Solatoroff. I visited with the Minkin sisters. I lived with my comrades Sasha and Fedya. You'll come with us, Helen?

HELEN: Who is us?

EMMA: Sasha and Fedya will come. Of course they will. Will you?

HELEN: I don't know.

EMMA: Of course you will. Your father is worse than my uncle. My aunt and uncle are nothing more than dull. I was in danger of nothing but falling asleep in my plate at their very dull dinners. Your father is a violent man.

This is true, but HELEN does not like to hear it.

HELEN: Emma, you exaggerate.

EMMA: He beats you. Doesn't he beat you?

HELEN: I don't wish to talk about it.

EMMA: I am your saviour, Helen. I give you an excuse to leave your father.

HELEN: Anna won't leave.

EMMA: Leave Anna. Your father is erotically fond of Anna.

HELEN: Emma!

EMMA: But he hates you, oddly enough.

HELEN: I don't want to discuss it, Emma!

EMMA: You mustn't think I speak frankly to hurt you.

HELEN: You do hurt me.

EMMA: It's because we're friends. We're comrades. We'll live together and work together. Come with us, Helen?

HELEN: I don't know.

EMMA: Do you love anarchy?

HELEN: Why is it that anarchists are always asking me if I love anarchy? I am always at meetings everlasting. I do nothing but listen to speeches. Of course I love anarchy. *(She bangs the cash box on the table to make her point)* And I've cut my hand on this box.

EMMA: I'm just asking.

HELEN: You ask too much sometimes.

EMMA: In Rochester, I followed the case of the Haymarket Martyrs in the newspapers. I went to hear Johanna Griei speak. After the meeting, she called me up to the platform. She told me that she'd watched my face as she spoke. She thought I must know the martyrs, I seemed to feel their tragedy so deeply. I said: "Unfortunately I do not know the men but I do feel the case with every fibre and when I heard you speak it seemed to me as if I knew them."

HELEN: You recite very dramatically, Emma.

EMMA: Do you know what she said to me?

HELEN: Something inspirational.

EMMA: She put her hand on my shoulder. "I have a feeling that you will know them better as you learn their ideal and that you will make their cause your own."

> *ALEXANDER BERKMAN enters to hear this last.*
> *FEDYA is with him.*

BERKMAN: I hope you do.

EMMA: I have, Sasha.

BERKMAN: Imperfectly.

HELEN: Look, Sasha. I cut my hand on the collection box.

EMMA: Look, Sasha, I dedicate my life to anarchy.

BERKMAN: I am committed. You are romantic.

EMMA: Johann Most doesn't think me romantic.

BERKMAN: Johann Most doesn't think of you at all, Emma. He is a very busy man.

EMMA: He is sending me to Rochester.

BERKMAN: To Rochester?

HELEN: But Sasha was supposed to go . . . Oh . . .

BERKMAN: It doesn't matter.

EMMA: I'm sorry, Sasha. I always speak too fast.

BERKMAN: No, I'm glad you told me. Johann Most will have his own reasons, of course.

FEDYA: He wants her in bed.

BERKMAN: Fedya!

FEDYA: It's true.

BERKMAN: I don't want to hear about it, Fedya!

EMMA: I'll kill you, Fedya!

> *EMMA is furious. She begins to chase FEDYA*
> *around the table.*

FEDYA: Look, Helen's finger is bleeding. Let me help you, Helen.

HELEN: It's all right.
FEDYA: You look faint, Helen. *(He picks her up and begins to carry her out of the room. To EMMA, as he exits)* You shouldn't strike a man with a woman in his arms.

> *EMMA is speechless with rage. ALEXANDER BERKMAN tries to comfort her.*

BERKMAN: Fedya is a moral cripple.

> *MOST has entered to watch this romping. He shouts. BERKMAN and EMMA make a fast exit.*

MOST: I cannot work in this confusion. Everything is chaos and I cannot work in chaos. My library is upside down. I find my own work . . . I find *The Science of Revolutionary Warfare* filed between Bakunin and Kropotkin. I cannot find my notes on the cloakmakers' strike. Emma! Emma! Emma!
EMMA: *(Re-enters)* Yes?
MOST: What have I written about the cloakmakers' strike?
EMMA: I don't know, Most.
MOST: And where have I written it?
EMMA: I don't know.
MOST: I can't work in this confusion.
EMMA: I don't blame you.
MOST: You will do me a kindness, Emma. You will pick up after me. Bring me peace and order.
EMMA: Me?
MOST: You will give me time for my work.
EMMA: You're much neater than I am.
MOST: Everything is chaos and I cannot work in chaos.
EMMA: You will clean it up.
MOST: You will clean it up.
EMMA:, You have an orderly nature.
MOST: *(Who has already begun to square things off)* That's true.
EMMA: And you know where everything goes.
MOST: *(Picking something up)* I want to ask you something.
EMMA: Ask me?

> *MOST uses picking things up to cover his confusion.*

MOST: Do my looks frighten you?
EMMA: No, of course not.
MOST: I'm disfigured, am I not? The beard doesn't disguise it. I look like a man who eats children.

EMMA: I never think of it.
MOST: Of course you do.
EMMA: Really.
MOST: My jaw. It's deformed.
EMMA: I don't think so.
MOST: Well, look at it.
EMMA: I see it, Hannes.
MOST: It is deformed.
EMMA: I see everything about you. You conceal nothing.
MOST: You think that?
EMMA: Yes, I do.
MOST: You don't notice my face . . . you say you don't and I
believe you . . .   (A pause. MOST will not be denied his theatrical
story)   I know what it looks like, however, if you do not. It's
come near to driving me to kill myself. Yes, "really." Before I
was old enough to grow this moustache. And once in prison
when they shaved my beard. My face is frightening.
EMMA: I don't notice your face. Or if I do, it seems beautiful.
Really.
MOST: I used to love the theatre. Schiller. I loved Schiller.
William Tell. I became obsessed with the idea that I could go on
the stage, play those tragedies. I went so far as to apply to a
theatre manager.
EMMA: And you acted?
MOST: He said I looked like a clown. Yes, because of my face.
A clown to play Schiller. Schiller as a Punch and Judy show.
Don't cry. Are you crying?

Of course she isn't crying.

EMMA: Yes I am.
MOST: I've been married twice. The marriages were failures.
Since I met you I've thought of that. I have a new obsession.
I thought if you needed me . . .
EMMA: I cannot go to Rochester, Most.
MOST: I was not talking about Rochester . . .
EMMA: I don't know the issues. I'm not ready . . .
MOST: We don't have to talk about Rochester now . . .
EMMA: Alexander Berkman has prepared himself for that
tour. Most . . . he knows the problems . . .
MOST: And I will not talk about Alexander Berkman!
EMMA: He understands the struggle for the eight hour day.
MOST: We are against that struggle. We don't have to under-
stand it.
EMMA: I could stay here in New York. I could work on the
cloakmakers' strike.

MOST: If you are my student, Emma . . . If you follow me, you can do anything. Do you believe that?
EMMA: I can do anything.
MOST: Be bold. Be arrogant. I am sure you will be brave.

They exit. KREIDERMAN and PARKS enter, bumping into FEDYA and HELEN who carry picket signs about the cloakmakers printed in Cyrillic characters. FEDYA and HELEN picket with some dignity.

KREIDERMAN: You people are violating a public ordinance the moment that your protest blocks the public right of way.
PARKS: Get a job!
KREIDERMAN: You live in a democracy now. That gives you the right of free speech. It does not give you the right to obstruct traffic.
PARKS: Get a job!
KREIDERMAN: This is a public thoroughfare. I mean to see that people continue to move along this street.
PARKS: Get a job!
KREIDERMAN: I think they have work, Parks. I think they are protesting the conditions in their various factories.
FRICK: *(Enters)* What's going on here?
KREIDERMAN: Anarchist street meeting, sir.
PARKS: Go back where you came from.
KREIDERMAN: Bolsheviks and their dupes, agitating against the free enterprise system.
PARKS: You people are asking for it.
KREIDERMAN: Foreigners, sir.
PARKS: That's right.
KREIDERMAN: Russkies and Krauts. Ivan and Hansel.
PARKS: Ask for it and you're going to get it.
FRICK: Can I get through?
PARKS: If you don't like it, stand up and fight for what you do like.
KREIDERMAN: See what you can do, Parks.

PARKS flourishes a bullwhip.

FRICK: You move on unarmed men and women with a bullwhip?
KREIDERMAN: There's no use talking to them, sir. We can't understand a word they say.
FRICK: Your enthusiasm is astonishing.

PARKS: Move along there. You heard me. I said move along, get moving. Make way for Mr. Frick . . . That means you as well. Move along, get moving . . .
FRICK: Give me your whip, Parks.
PARKS: Beg your pardon, sir?
KREIDERMAN: Give Mr. Frick your whip, Mr. Parks.
FRICK: This isn't Mother Russia. We do not horsewhip the peasants in New York.
PARKS: Talking their language, sir.
FRICK: Teach them our language.

Exit FRICK.

PARKS: *(To FEDYA)*   See that line. Step over that line. I dare you. Come on and get what's coming to you.
KREIDERMAN: Henry Clay Frick is a fine man. He's a captain of industry.
PARKS: *(To FEDYA)*   I'm not going to waste my breath asking you twice, you godless, murdering Bolshevik. I dare you. Step over that line.
KREIDERMAN: He's probably meeting Mr. Andrew Carnegie, the philanthropist who owns the Homestead Steel Mills. But he still has time to give us his advice.
PARKS: All right, you yellow-bellied, yellow-livered Red, if you aren't going to step over here, I'm going over there to get you.
KREIDERMAN: *(Sharply)*   Parks!
PARKS: Yes, sir.
KREIDERMAN: Teach them our language.

> *FEDYA turns to see what KREIDERMAN is saying. KREIDERMAN escorts HELEN offstage. PARKS clips FEDYA behind the ear and beats him down to the ground. MOST enters to deliver a speech to the audience.*

MOST: Know your enemy. It is capitalism. It is the capitalistic system. Capitalism denies your humanity. Capitalism's greatest achievement, capitalism's crowning glory is the assembly line. The assembly line binds a man, a free man, to a machine. For up to fourteen hours a day the man serves the machine and the machine creates material wealth. The man serves the system and the system cages the man. We know that men are free. We know we can act. It is you who must act. We will act to free our brothers. It is the individual act of a free man that is creative. It is by the individual acts of free men that we progress. Attentat!

PARKS aims his foot for one last kick. Blackout.

Lights up on HELEN, wrapped in a blanket, sitting at the table in the anarchists' commune. EMMA enters, very happy.

EMMA: Good morning, Helen.
HELEN: Don't say anything. Don't say anything more.
EMMA: We are free and the morning is bright.
HELEN: You are free. I am tired.
EMMA: You look tired.
HELEN: Yes, I am.
EMMA: You didn't sleep well.
HELEN: Not at all.
EMMA: *(Glorious)* Neither did I.
HELEN: I know that.
EMMA: We woke you. We kept you up. Is that what you're trying to tell me?
HELEN: I'll take a leaf from your book, Emma. I'll confess something to you. When I am lying in a very narrow bed somewhat cold and almost damp, I am not amused by whispers and chuckles, by heavy breathing and theatrical groans, I am not amused by carols of joy from the room next door. You know when the sun rose this morning, Emma, I think you woke Sasha to tell him about it, do you remember? I did not share your happiness.
EMMA: We disturbed you.
HELEN: It is jealousy. I admit it. I see that I am weak and mean. Mean and weak, Oh God. I see why you do it, Emma. I see why you flay yourself with every emotion that flickers through your eyes. This is marvellous. Oh God, she said, she tore her hair, she tore open her waist. She fainted. *(FEDYA enters, shirtless, wrapped in another blanket. There is a large bruise on his chest)* Look, Fedya. I have learned from Emma. Self expression. I have freed my emotions. I am playing at being Emma and I have shut her up. I have finally shut her up.
FEDYA: I see that.
EMMA: What's the matter with Helen?
FEDYA: What did you say to her?
EMMA: I said "Good morning, Helen."
FEDYA: Your enthusiasm is infectious.
BERKMAN: *(Enters, looking the worse for wear)* Good morning all.
HELEN: Dance with me, Sasha.
BERKMAN: I want four cups of coffee and a long rest.

152

HELEN: Dance with me, Sasha. While the dawn comes silently. Till the sun streams in the window and warms us. I can see the dawn on your skin, Sasha.
BERKMAN: You told her.
EMMA: Me? She overheard.
FEDYA: We overheard.
EMMA: You want some toast, Sasha?
FEDYA: The neighbourhood overheard, I suppose. Emma is not discreet.
EMMA: I am really hungry this morning.
FEDYA: How about you, Sasha?
BERKMAN: What do you mean?
FEDYA: Are you really hungry this morning?
BERKMAN: You insinuate.
FEDYA: I ask about your appetite.
BERKMAN: I'm getting out of here.
FEDYA: Eh, Dushenka?
HELEN: Oh, Dushenka! Dance with me, Dushenka!
FEDYA: Kiss me, Dushenka. Because tomorrow I go to Rochester.
HELEN: Will you miss me while I am in Rochester, Dushenka?
BERKMAN: Where's my hat? Where's my scarf?
EMMA: Be a good sport, Sasha.
BERKMAN: Where are my boots?
FEDYA: Be a good sport, Dushenka. Helen and I, we are both good sports.
EMMA: Come on, dance. We'll all dance.
BERKMAN: Sure we'll dance. And Emma will practice public speaking. As she did last night. So when she goes to Rochester, she'll make sure she's heard.
HELEN: Dushenka! Dushenka! Dushenka!
EMMA: Wait a minute, Sasha, I'll go with you.
BERKMAN: No.
EMMA: I don't mind. I'll just get my coat.

They exit in opposite directions.

HELEN: Johann Most is a man of some sensitivity, Fedya, is he not?
FEDYA: I'm going back to bed.
HELEN: *(Following him)* He'll see Emma for what she is. He'll see how silly she is.

They exit. Enter FRICK, KREIDERMAN and PARKS. KREIDERMAN and PARKS in ludicrous disguises.

FRICK: I hope you men are here with open minds.

PARKS: Yes, sir.

KREIDERMAN: Interesting to hear the other side. See the other fellow's point of view.

PARKS: Yes, sir.

KREIDERMAN: We like to be reasonable. That's our training. We're Pinkerton men.

>   *EMMA enters and mounts the speaker's podium. She seems to begin to speak although we don't hear anything.*

PARKS: What did she say?

FRICK: Fellow workers.

PARKS: Speaking some foreign language.

KREIDERMAN: She's speaking German.

PARKS: That's what I said.

FRICK: She's talking about the struggle for the eight hour day.

PARKS: Do you understand German, sir?

KREIDERMAN: Mr. Frick has travelled extensively. In Europe.

PARKS: Does he understand German, I'm asking him.

FRICK: Yes. I do.

PARKS: Do you understand what she's saying, sir?

KREIDERMAN: It's in German, isn't it?

PARKS: That's what I'm asking him.

FRICK: She's talking about the struggle for the eight hour day.

KREIDERMAN: Make a note of that, Parks.

PARKS: *(To KREIDERMAN)*   Is it subversive, sir?

>   *They join applause which seems to be going on about them.*

KREIDERMAN: What's all the cheering for? I don't understand a word she's saying.

PARKS: Bunch of foreigners here. They all speak German.

KREIDERMAN: *(To FRICK)*   Is it subversive, sir?

>   *Lights up full on EMMA.*

EMMA: In the past, we've asked you to fight with us for the eight hour day. Now I've come to ask you to stop that fight. We have something bigger to do. We must work together to destroy the capitalist system.

Here in Rochester, we have been concerned with the eight hour day. In Pennsylvania, at the Homestead Steel Mills, the workers ask for higher wages and the right to organize.

Sometimes we see no further than our own small concerns. We can't understand that as long as Andrew Carnegie owns the product of our labour, as long as Henry Clay Frick works for Andrew Carnegie, and we work for Henry Clay Frick, it doesn't matter how long we work or how much we are paid. *(KREIDERMAN and PARKS cheer at the sound of these familiar names. HENRY CLAY FRICK tries to silence them)* As long as Andrew Carnegie owns us, the world is horribly wrong. We must change the world. *(FRICK and the Pinkerton men are unmoved)* Until we own the factories, our work will be drudgery. When we own the factories, our work will be joy. All of us work fourteen, sixteen hours every day for the cause. We have dedicated our life to the cause and the work is our joy. We have no concern for personal comfort. We will work as long as we must. We will not stop working until we reach our goal.

> *KREIDERMAN and PARKS cheer, carried away by oratory and occasion. FRICK waves his hand in the air.*

FRICK: Excuse me . . . my friends don't understand your point.
EMMA: *(To FRICK)*   Are you factory workers?
FRICK: I wonder if politicians ever think that their talk directs our lives. I wonder if you know how easy it is for you to talk of abandoning the struggle for the eight hour day. Those who work each day for ten hours or twelve hours or fourteen hours. Those who have spent their lives in a mill and want nothing but a few hours every day in peace. They will be glad to talk philosophy with you.
EMMA: Do you work in a mill?
FRICK: It doesn't matter.
EMMA: Who are you?
FRICK: It doesn't matter who I am if I'm telling you the truth.
EMMA: I tell the truth.
PARKS: Kreiderman?
KREIDERMAN: What, Parks?
PARKS: You think she's one of those suffragettes?

> *PARKS and KREIDERMAN are giggling and leering.*

EMMA: What about your friends. What about you? How do you feel? You are working men. I'm talking to you.
FRICK: You will excuse my friends.

PARKS: Hey, Cookie . . . (*As EMMA turns toward him*)
Not you, hard tack.
FRICK: They are going back to work. Come Parks. Kreiderman.
EMMA: I explain myself so badly. My English is poor. But you
speak German, perhaps you could explain . . .

> *They exit. EMMA follows. BERKMAN, HELEN and
> FEDYA prepare to welcome EMMA home. They
> enter and the scene becomes the* Freiheit *office.*

BERKMAN: Do you have the banner?
HELEN: Do you think Emma will like that banner? What if she
sees the other side?
BERKMAN: The other side is "Remember the Haymarket
Martyrs."
HELEN: It seems impersonal.
FEDYA: Sasha would say it's a fine revolutionary sentiment.
BERKMAN: Sasha would say it isn't enough.

> *EMMA enters, very downcast, in time to hear this
> last.*

EMMA: No, of course not.
FEDYA: Welcome home, Emma.
BERKMAN: We came to make sure Johann Most put headlines
in his newspaper. "Emma . . . The Girl . . . Comes Home."
EMMA: Words aren't enough. Words are never enough. Words
are meaningless.
FEDYA: You're a success, Emma. A huge success.
HELEN: Everybody cheering. All the crowds.
EMMA: It was awful, Sasha.
BERKMAN: Fedya has composed a song on the condition that
Helen and I will sing it. I indulge myself.
EMMA: I am very ignorant.

> *They sing "a capella."*

Welcome Emma, Queen of the Anarchists
Had you been gone much longer
We might have slashed our wrists.

FEDYA: Sasha has allowed me to buy you flowers. Here it is.

> *He presents EMMA with a bushy potted plant.*

BERKMAN: I chose the flower. For you, Emma.

EMMA: Johann wants to talk to me.
BERKMAN: Fedya says it is a good sturdy plant. I see it is
practical. I want it to be more than that.
FEDYA: Johann Wurst wants to talk to you. That's his name.
Johann Sausage.
BERKMAN: Take your flower.

MOST enters carrying violets.

BERKMAN: What is that?
MOST: Violets.
BERKMAN: It is the middle of winter, Emma and he gives
you violets.
MOST: You see she has taken the violets and you are left
holding that colourful tree.
BERKMAN: Thousands of people out of work and hungry and
he gives you violets.
MOST: Alexander Berkman does not have a generous spirit.
BERKMAN: I do not indulge myself at the expense of others.
MOST: You attack me. That is an indulgence.
BERKMAN: Violets are stupid. Useless. Extravagant.
MOST: You resent Emma's success.
BERKMAN: I do not.
MOST: That is why you are angry. That is why you attack me.
BERKMAN: I attack you because you are wrong.
MOST: You see yourself as a spokesman for anarchy.
BERKMAN: And I am.
MOST: Your dreary philosophy is anarchy.
BERKMAN: My philosophy is clearly reasoned. It is sane and
humanistic.
MOST: You have no imagination.
BERKMAN: Of course I do not take theatrical poses.
MOST: You do make rules for anarchists, however.
BERKMAN: I do not dramatize myself until I'm a figure of fun.
MOST: Anarchy is a living force above your rules.
BERKMAN: I do not see myself as a character in a cheap
melodrama.
MOST: I see myself in Schiller tragedies, Berkman. I see you as
a political puppet.
BERKMAN: Violets. Cheap theatrics. You are an old man
dreaming of romances on the barricades. Emma will not play in
your romance.
MOST: And here is the tragic Anna Minkin.
HELEN: I'm Helen. Minkin.
MOST: So you are.
HELEN: Anna is my sister.

MOST: It was seeing you with Berkman. Berkman and Anna Minkin. They are inseparable I had understood.
BERKMAN: Emma says that she must talk to you.
MOST: Then no doubt you will leave Emma here to talk.
BERKMAN: If she wishes.
MOST: And you will return to Anna Minkin. Since you are so seldom apart.
BERKMAN: We did not come here to discuss where I go or what I do.
MOST: Certainly not. Because here we discuss anarchy. We dedicate our lives to anarchy. We are not self-seeking young men chasing silly young women.
BERKMAN: I will ask you to be brief, Emma.
MOST: I will ask you to leave my office.
BERKMAN: Who?
MOST: As she has told you, Emma and I have business to discuss.
BERKMAN: But not alone.
MOST: Yes.
BERKMAN: She'll come with me.
EMMA: No, Sasha.
BERKMAN: Yes, you will.
EMMA: I won't.
BERKMAN: I think Johann Most believes that man does not need law or government or authority because he feels man has some special strength.
MOST: That's correct.
BERKMAN: There are others and I count myself among them, who want individual autonomy because man is inherently good. You pervert every principle of revolution. You lead the revolution because you want the power. You want to be anarchist king. Come Fedya, Helen.

They exit.

MOST: I have brought you flowers. Violets.
EMMA: I want to tell you about the tour.
MOST: I know about the tour. Do you like them?
EMMA: What happened in Rochester . . .
MOST: You were eloquent in Rochester . . .
EMMA: It went very badly.
MOST: You were entertaining in Buffalo. In Cleveland you entered an entirely new arena. Anarchy became a popular attraction.
EMMA: That's what you printed in *Freiheit*. Do you want to know what I felt?

MOST: Of course I do. Another time.
EMMA: Now.
MOST: We have been apart for two weeks, Emma.
EMMA: You were wrong, Most.
MOST: Agreed. We will not be apart again.
EMMA: About the struggle for the eight hour day.
MOST: I don't want to talk about the eight hour day.
EMMA: I do.
MOST: Don't be silly, Emma.
EMMA: I will not be treated like a silly woman. You sent me out to speak for you like a trained dog. I've made a fool of myself. I didn't speak for myself, I said your words. I've said pretentious, pompous things. There are men who work fourteen hours a day. I spoke to them. One man came up after my lecture, Johann. Grey-headed, his hands shook. He had spent his life on a factory assembly line, Johann, and I learned more from his simple words than from all your books. You care only for the symmetry of your world. You only want your philosophy secure.
MOST: Viper.
EMMA: If you worked in a factory fourteen hours a day . . .
MOST: Snake!
EMMA: Breathing foul air, cramped in a space beside a machine.
MOST: I taught you everything!
EMMA: I'm only telling you what I feel.
MOST: You've betrayed me.
EMMA: I speak for you but I will not say your words.
MOST: You're like everybody else. I would rather cut you out of my heart altogether than have you as a lukewarm friend . . . who is not with me, is against me! I would not have it other-wise. I gave you my mystery and you ate it!
EMMA: I think for myself! I speak for myself! Johann!

MOST storms out. FEDYA enters, since he has been listening at the door.

FEDYA: Johann Wurst has eaten his violets.
EMMA: Fedya . . .
FEDYA: Are you all right?
EMMA: Yes.
FEDYA: You look like you're going to cry.
EMMA: I'm not crying.

But she is. FEDYA holds her.

FEDYA: If I were going to paint you . . .

EMMA: Will you paint me?

FEDYA: I am not a painter, Emma. I do crayon enlargements for a commercial artist. I do advertising.

EMMA: If you paint me, will it be a nude?

FEDYA: No.

EMMA: Why not?

FEDYA: You're ready to pose in the nude, I suppose?

EMMA: Of course.

FEDYA: If I paint you, Emma, you will not look like a statue in a public park.

EMMA: Why not?

FEDYA: I am an artist.

EMMA: There is nothing wrong with nudity.

FEDYA: I love you, Emma. I take your nudity seriously. I take your tears seriously but you aren't crying anymore. Sometimes I wish you were vulnerable, Emma. Sometimes I wish you were mysterious. Do you know what that means?

EMMA: *(Nonplussed)* Are you a pre-Raphaelite?

FEDYA: Do I look like a pre-Raphaelite?

EMMA: Well, I don't know what a pre-Raphaelite looks like.

FEDYA: You'll be all right, won't you? You'll be in a union hall tomorrow, organizing somebody. You're very strong and healthy.

> *HELEN and BERKMAN enter to join in the song and dance.*

The cloakmakers' bosses
Say their striking workers
Should not have the right
To fight to be free
The cloakmakers' bosses
Depend on our labour
They cannot continue
Without you and me

If helping your sisters
Is what you would like
Come to the dance
For the cloakmakers' strike.

> *EMMA climbs on a table to speak. She is more confident and more convincing than before.*

EMMA: Women's emancipation? How much independence is gained if the narrowness and lack of freedom of the home is exchanged for the narrowness and lack of freedom of the factory, sweat shops, department store or office?

Why should I join a union? I am going to get married and have a home. Have you not been taught from infancy to look upon that as your ultimate calling? You learn soon enough that the home, though not as large a prison as the factory, has more solid doors and bars.

The song continues.

The Cloakmakers' Union
As strong as its members
And strong as its members
Means like you and me
And fighting together
Means winning our battles
So our lives will be
What we want them to be

If helping your sisters
Is what you would like
Come to the dance for
The cloakmakers' strike.

EMMA: Woman's development, her freedom, her independence must come from and through herself. First by asserting herself as a personality, and not as a sex commodity. Second by refusing the right to anyone over her body, by refusing to bear children unless she wants them, by refusing to be a servant to God, the state, society and husband, the family. By making her life simpler, but deeper and richer. That is, by trying to learn the meaning and substance of life in all its complexities, by freeing herself from the fear of public opinion and public condemnation. Only that will set woman free, will make her a force hitherto unknown in the world, a force of real love, for peace, for harmony — a force of divine fire, of life-giving, a creator of free men and women.

The song continues.

The Cloakmakers' Union
Is standing together
The bosses will listen
The bosses will see
That we stand united
Our voices are strong

And the Cloakmakers' Union
Will make us all free

If helping your sisters
Is what you would like
Come to the dance for
The cloakmakers' strike.

Blackout.

Act Two

A small table has been added to the upper level. The speaker's podium has been moved to the lower level.

KREIDERMAN discovers PARKS working in FRICK's office on the upper level. He gives him a Cossack hat.

KREIDERMAN: Mr. Frick is appearing tonight in *The Assassination of Alexander II.*
PARKS: Yes, sir.
KREIDERMAN: At the Philadelphia Light Opera Society. It's a benefit performance for charity.
PARKS: Yes, sir.
KREIDERMAN: You're playing a Cossack.
PARKS: But sir, I can't do that. I couldn't appear on the stage.
KREIDERMAN: You will do it. There is a spectacular effect in the assassination scene. The Czar's sleigh pulled by his famous team of matched greys has been blown apart by the bomb of the conspirator Rysakov. The Czar steps from the carriage. Thank God you're all right, sir, says the Cossack.
PARKS: *(Sings)* Thank God you're all right, sir.
KREIDERMAN: Yes, I'm all right, thank God, sings the Czar. The conspirator Grevevitsky steps from the crowd. His hands above his head. It's too soon to thank God, he sings. He walks right up to the Czar and drops his bomb directly between them. Boom! The Czar's right leg is blown off. Above his waist his body is an unrecognizable mass of blood.

KREIDERMAN exits. FRICK enters dressed as Czar Alexander II.

FRICK: *(Sings)*
Emperor of all the Russias
Ruler of a mighty nation
Statesman Judge and King and Czar
Working for emancipation
All reforms come from the Czar
Reforms come from above

163

That way though the serfs are free
And Russia lives in liberty
Russia still will always be
The Russia that we love
BUT
Though everyone sings praises
And advisors may applaud
Remember it is hard to be
An instrument of God.

> *FRICK and PARKS exit to huge rounds of applause. FEDYA, HELEN and EMMA enter the anarchists' commune.*

FEDYA: I am going to paint an epic canvas. The Imperial Family. The Czar Alexander II as he freed the serfs. Helen will pose as the Empress . . . Here Helen, hold this. Pretend it's a Fabergé Egg.
EMMA: The Czar and the Empress will be shown as little people in the background of the canvas. They will be overwhelmed by the tide of events. In the foreground, there will be a serf, free and noble. I will pose for that figure.
FEDYA: Alexander frees the serfs. It will be a series.
HELEN: What will I wear, Fedya?
EMMA: There will be a wind. It will blow my hair back. There will be an aura of golden light around my face.

> *BERKMAN enters. He is not amused.*

BERKMAN: And behind you there will be a line of dancing workers.
HELEN: Come and stand beside me, Sasha. Be in Fedya's picture.
BERKMAN: There are some books that I should have.
HELEN: Come and be Alexander II.
BERKMAN: *(Horrified)* Alexander II?
HELEN: Alexander frees the serfs. It's history.
FEDYA: It's an advertising campaign.
BERKMAN: You are a traitor to our class, Fedya.
FEDYA: It's a public service. To sell sardines.
BERKMAN: Alexander II freed the serfs because he feared the will of the people. He was a spineless worm. My uncle Maxim hanged the Cossacks. That's history.
EMMA: Sasha and Fedya arrive in New York. Friendless. Without money. They huddle together in a doorway as the wind whistles. As the snow blows. That's history.

164

BERKMAN: I will not tax you with this stupidity, Emma. I try not to criticize, although we are so different.

EMMA: Because I want freedom, the right to self-expression, everybody's right to be beautiful, radiant things.

BERKMAN: I live austerely. With my philosophy. You do not. You like to romp.

EMMA: To what?

BERKMAN: To romp. You know. Your sense of fun.

EMMA: How is Anna Minkin, Sasha?

HELEN: Sasha and Anna are living together.

EMMA: All right! I know!

FEDYA: Emma . . . calm yourself.

EMMA: I'm sorry. I scream at you. I turn on my closest companion. It is an emotional indulgence. Forgive me, Helen. It is not your fault if Sasha lives with your silly sister.

HELEN: Anna is a very quiet woman.

EMMA: Sasha needs peace. Of course.

HELEN: They speak of having a family.

EMMA: Anna speaks.

HELEN: And Sasha. He wants children. He wants peace.

> *EMMA now begins to build to a hysterical scene. HELEN, FEDYA and BERKMAN have seen it all before, hundreds of times. They are bored. BERKMAN reads. FEDYA sketches HELEN.*

EMMA: I can never have children.

FEDYA: Emma . . .

EMMA: I can never have children. I suffer. Sometimes I suffer unbearable pain. When I first came to New York, I discussed my complaint with Solatoroff who took me to a doctor.

BERKMAN: Emma, you dramatize yourself again.

EMMA: The specialists urged an operation. He was surprised that I had been able to stand my condition so long. He said I would never be free from pain. I would never experience full sexual release, unless I submitted to the operation.

HELEN: Heaven forbid that your sexual release should not be full.

EMMA: He said I could never bear children. I love children madly.

FEDYA: You'll make yourself sick, Emma.

EMMA: I love babies passionately but I remember my own childhood. My father wanted a boy. The pig woman had brought me instead, he told me. The pig woman had cheated him. Perhaps if I were very sick, perhaps if I were dying he would be kind.

FEDYA: You're raving, Emma.
EMMA: No child of mine will be unwanted. No child of mine will be unloved. I won't have a child. I will live for my ideal. I will suffer for my ideal. I will not have the operation.
FEDYA: She's going to faint.
HELEN: She's always going to faint.

EMMA faints. FEDYA and BERKMAN catch her.

FEDYA: Help me with her, Sasha.
EMMA: Fedya and I are lovers, Sasha.
FEDYA: She's raving.
EMMA: It's true, isn't it?
BERKMAN: It's true, isn't it?
FEDYA: Of course it's true. But she doesn't know what she's saying, Sasha.
BERKMAN: Emma, listen to me. The catechism of the Russian Revolution says the revolutionary must give up his home, his parents, his lover, his children, everything. I agree with that absolutely. But I do love you. I wanted you to know that.

FEDYA has tried to ease EMMA back to the table.
BERKMAN leans over to kiss EMMA. She's
enthusiastic. FEDYA tries to extricate himself
from their embrace.

HELEN: She has fooled you again. All she has to do is scream and faint.
EMMA: Helen, you must calm yourself.
HELEN: Of course you and Fedya are only boys. You cannot help your immaturity. A man of more experience, of more intelligence, a man like Johann Most would not be taken in.
BERKMAN: Johann Most? Johann Most has had her name carved on his chest.
HELEN: You are very stupid, Sasha, if you think Most concerns himself with a silly girl.
BERKMAN: He has made a career of it.
HELEN: You show how small you are when you mock him.
FEDYA: Why is Helen so concerned with Most?
HELEN: I love him.
FEDYA: Go and make some popcorn, Helen.
HELEN: I love Most.
FEDYA: Stay home tonight, Helen. Rest. Drink plenty of liquid.
HELEN: I love him.
EMMA: I knew it.

HELEN: You knew it! Of course, you know everything!

FEDYA: What is Sasha doing?

EMMA: Helen . . .

HELEN: Perhaps one thing you do not know . . . I can make Johann Most happy if you cannot . . .

EMMA: I have offended you, Helen. I see that. I know how you feel.

HELEN: You do not.

FEDYA: What are you doing Sasha?

BERKMAN: I'm moving this table.

EMMA: I can tell you about Hannes, Helen . . .

HELEN: I will go to hear him. I will go anywhere he speaks. I will follow him from one engagement to another.

EMMA: You're very foolish, Helen.

HELEN: You think you're very clever and you think I'm very stupid and you think I don't know what you think.

FEDYA: This is our table.

BERKMAN: I need it for my work.

BERKMAN and FEDYA carry the table out. It's necessary to clear the lower stage area for the trial scene.

EMMA: Be quiet, Sasha.

HELEN: You think no one understands anything but you . . . you understand everything, you love everything, you have everything.

EMMA: I will go to Hannes because I know him better than you do. You are wrong to think he is mature, Helen. He is very impressionable. He is weak with women.

EMMA exits.

HELEN: I don't want your help. I don't want your help! She thinks she can do anything. She can save me. She can save the world. She can scream louder than I can.

HELEN exits. Enter FRICK, KREIDERMAN and PARKS on the upper level.

PARKS: What are you going to tell the union at Homestead, Mr. Frick?

FRICK: Union?

KREIDERMAN: Mr. Frick doesn't recognize the union, Mr. Parks.

FRICK: I won't negotiate, I'll propose a twenty-two per cent wage cut throughout the mill. I'll put that on their bargaining table.
PARKS: What will they say to that, sir?
FRICK: I don't sit at their bargaining table, Parks. I don't know what they say and I don't care.

They exit. Enter MOST and EMMA.

EMMA: Helen Minkin says she loves you.
MOST: Helen is available. I know that, of course.
EMMA: Tell me what you feel for her.
MOST: Nothing.
EMMA: She loves you.
MOST: I think Helen's passion is largely sexual.
EMMA: I don't see the difference.
MOST: Love isn't sex. Sex isn't love.
EMMA: They are inseparable.
MOST: Not in Helen's case.
EMMA: For any woman.
MOST: She thinks she loves me. I am sure any other man would do as well.
EMMA: Helen is not often in hysterics.
MOST: Is she not?
EMMA: You are either cruel or stupid.
MOST: Have her try that arrogant Russian Jew.
EMMA: Who?
MOST: Your friend. Your young fool.
EMMA: I am a Russian Jew, Most.
MOST: I said arrogant. He is arrogant.
EMMA: He is inspired.
MOST: He tells me about revolutionary ethics.
EMMA: Why not?
MOST: He knows nothing of life. He bores me.
EMMA: Many things bore you. It's why you bore me sometimes.
MOST: And he offends me.
EMMA: You are talking rubbish.
MOST: You will have to choose between us.
EMMA: There's no choice for me in an idiot who thinks all women are fools.
MOST: I think Helen is a fool.
EMMA: Who dares to say he wants me all to himself. Who treats me like an object he can own.
MOST: Choose Berkman then.
EMMA: Of course I will.
MOST: Choose your beautiful mindless boy.

168

EMMA: Choose my arrogant Russian jew.
MOST: Yes.
EMMA: Sasha knows women and he knows you.
MOST: Sasha! Who is Sasha? Children!
EMMA: He says you're no longer an anarchist. He says you're
a posturing cripple.
MOST: Calling names.
EMMA: He is right.
MOST: AAAAhhh!

MOST screams and falls at her feet.

EMMA: Most? Most?

*EMMA is very tentative. Very embarrassed. FRICK
appears.*

FRICK: Get up! Get up!
EMMA: Get up, Most.
FRICK: That looks like very "disorderly" conduct.
EMMA: Will you go away? Will you mind your own business?
FRICK: An old man and a young girl "making love" in the
street? Someone should call a policeman.
EMMA: What do you want a policeman for?
FRICK: To maintain order.
EMMA: Get up, Most.
MOST: No, I won't.
FRICK: Officer?

PARKS appears.

EMMA: *(To MOST)* If they recognize you. They're police.
If they know who you are . . .
MOST: The King of the Anarchists dying of love in the streets
of New York.
FRICK: Excuse me, officer . . .
MOST: Excuse me, officer. Take me to prison. I'll go back to
Blackwell's Island. It is the Inquisition brought to American
soil.
EMMA: Excuse me, officer, my father has had a sudden attack
of dizziness.
FRICK: Are you trying to tell a New York policeman that
man is your father?
EMMA: Why not?
FRICK: He won't believe that. Will you?
PARKS: No, sir.

EMMA: My father is very ill. If you could run for a doctor.
FRICK: What your father should do is give the policeman five dollars. I would. In the unlikely event that the policeman had found me "grovelling" in the street with a child. "Disturbing the peace," so to speak.
MOST: Bribery.
FRICK: As I said. Five dollars.
MOST: I won't pay bribes. Take me.
EMMA: I'll give you five dollars.
MOST: I'm not her father. Believe me. I am her lover. She is rejecting me.
EMMA: Here. Take the money. Pay him. I'll take my father home.
MOST: I'm not your father.
FRICK: If he is her father, he has unhealthy passions. Perhaps ten dollars.
EMMA: Come on, Most.
FRICK: What do you think officer? Shall we make sure the aged gentleman reaches his home safely?
PARKS: Perhaps fifteen dollars.
FRICK: Twenty?
PARKS: Twenty-five.

> *The bids escalate as they exit. FEDYA enters and sings "The Song of the Homestead Strike." During his song, BERKMAN and EMMA enter.*

FEDYA: *(Sings)*
Henry Clay Frick hated unions with passion
The Steelworkers' Union worked militantly
Frick said to his boss, Mr. Andrew Carnegie
Go off to Scotland and leave it to me

Widows and orphans evicted and tricked
At the hands of the villainous Henry Clay Frick

Henry Clay Frick told the strikers at Homestead
He'd see them dead rather than bargain again
Six of them died on the banks of the river
Shot without cause by his Pinkerton men

Widows and orphans evicted and tricked
At the hands of the villainous Henry Clay Frick

Pinkertons hired to guard Homestead Steel Mills
Strikebreakers hired to help keep things hot
Pinkertons fired on unarmed steelworkers
A nine-year-old boy was the first man shot

Widows and orphans evicted and tricked
At the hands of the villanous Henry Clay Frick.

BERKMAN: I must go to Homestead.
FEDYA: Alexander Berkman fights the forces of oppression.
BERKMAN: Henry Clay Frick is a cold-blooded murderer.
He's responsible for the deaths. He must take the consequences.
FEDYA: There are no consequences.
BERKMAN: There will be.
FEDYA: He owns the police.
BERKMAN: That is why, in anarchism, we speak of the
individual act. Read Most. Read *Science of Revolutionary
Warfare.*
FEDYA: Don't quote Most to me. You aren't even speaking to
him.
BERKMAN: He taught all of us. He told me what to do.
FEDYA: You're crazy, Sasha.
BERKMAN: I will act against Frick.
FEDYA: No you won't. You're crazy.
BERKMAN: I want to accomplish an act of significance.
FEDYA: Well you won't.
BERKMAN: I will assassinate Henry Clay Frick.
FEDYA: I knew you were going to say that. I knew you were
crazy.
BERKMAN: It is an Attentat.
FEDYA: You think if you kill Frick, that all across the
country people will rise up and throw off the laws and the
systems that make them slaves.
BERKMAN: Propaganda of the deed.
FEDYA: Well, they won't. Nothing will happen. Except Frick
will be dead and you will be dead. No one will listen, Sasha. If
you kill Frick, they will kill you.
BERKMAN: I know that. I must act.
FEDYA: No.
EMMA: We are anarchists, Fedya.
FEDYA: We are friends.
BERKMAN: Insufferable bourgeois.
FEDYA: Don't call me names.
BERKMAN: Mindless capitalist lackey.
FEDYA: I'm trying to talk sense to you.
BERKMAN: Sentimental reactionary coward.
FEDYA: You are dangerous.
BERKMAN: A political assassination.
FEDYA: You're out of your mind.
EMMA: I'll help you, Sasha.
BERKMAN: I'll make a bomb. With a time regulator.

FEDYA: Now you're talking like Most.

BERKMAN: I know that.

FEDYA: Individual act of violence. Attentat. *The Science of Revolutionary Warfare*. Chapter 4, "Blowing up a Capitalist."

BERKMAN: So I can kill Frick and save myself. Because I'll kill him, I'll be captured, no, I'll give myself up. And of course, I'll be condemned to death. But I'll speak in court before I die. I'll speak in court and I'll kill myself.

EMMA: And the people will know you aren't a criminal.

BERKMAN: The people will know I'm an idealist.

FEDYA: *(Sings reprise)*

He knows he must find a significant act
He makes the decision with terrible calm
Consider the case of Henry Clay Frick
The murderer dies by an anarchist's bomb

Widows and orphans evicted and tricked
At the hands of the villainous Henry Clay Frick.

> *At the end of the song, BERKMAN is working over his bombs.*

BERKMAN: I don't want you here, Emma.

EMMA: Why not?

BERKMAN: Because I am testing the bomb, of course. Because I must see its effect. I have two bombs and I set this one off to learn how I may best use the other.

EMMA: Right. We must see its effect.

BERKMAN: I'll tell you about it.

EMMA: After the events in Chicago, Louis Lingg blew himself up with his own bomb and on the wall, in his own blood, he wrote "Long live anarchy." As he died.

BERKMAN: Get out of here.

EMMA: You have the bomb in the sand pit. Let me watch.

BERKMAN: Go find Fedya.

EMMA: There. I lit the fuse.

> *BERKMAN pulls her away from the bomb.*

BERKMAN: Get down. *(As FEDYA enters)* Watch out, Fedya. We have lit the fuse.

> *FEDYA falls flat. BERKMAN pushes EMMA down and falls on top of her. A pause until the bomb's fuse fizzles out.*

FEDYA: The bomb is silent. It is useful for clandestine work.
BERKMAN: Very funny.
FEDYA: Henry Clay Frick won't know he's been killed.
EMMA: What happened? What went wrong?
BERKMAN: The dynamite was too damp. The directions were wrong . . . I don't know.
FEDYA: It didn't go off. All right. It's over.
EMMA: What about the other bomb?
BERKMAN: It won't work either.
EMMA: Why not? Of course it will.
BERKMAN: I went to some trouble to make them exactly the same.
EMMA: It won't go off?
BERKMAN: I have another plan. I need a gun. I need the money to get a gun.
EMMA: Go to Johann Most.
BERKMAN: He won't help us.
EMMA: He will. He'll help me.
BERKMAN: I need a gun. I need a suit of clothes so I can present myself at Frick's office.
FEDYA: I won't help you.
EMMA: I can get the money, Sasha. We can go to Homestead.
FEDYA: You aren't going, Emma.
EMMA: I could be the first one in Frick's office. I could say I was skilled at the typewriter. I could carry a small handbag to conceal the gun.
BERKMAN: You aren't going.
FEDYA: Emma isn't crazy enough to go. Sasha is the one who thinks he can walk in and murder a man.

Exit FEDYA.

EMMA: Of course I'm going.
BERKMAN: I don't have time to argue with you, Emma.
EMMA: I don't want to argue. I believe in this act, absolutely. I want to go to Homestead and I will go.
BERKMAN: We do not go to Homestead because we "want" to go. Each of us has responsibility. You will get the money for me. Get Johann Most. I'll talk to him. Go Emma. Please. Go now.

EMMA exits. BERKMAN is left alone on the lower level. Enter KREIDERMAN and FRICK on the upper level.

FRICK: I didn't ask for strikebreakers, Kreiderman, I asked for police.

KREIDERMAN: The Pinkerton Detective Agency, sir . . .

FRICK: I wanted order. And we had a war.

KREIDERMAN: It was the strikers, sir. Look, sir, we were trying to land in barges from across the Monongahela, but those people had a homemade cannon, sir. They had fire bombs. They wanted to blow those barges out of the water, sir, so one of our men opened fire and then he . . .

FRICK: I suppose your man was mad with fear.

KREIDERMAN: Yes, sir.

FRICK: That one man, Kreiderman. Who lost his head. Since he was mad with fear. He and his single police special killed one nine-year-old boy and five strikers. In pitch darkness from a barge in the middle of the Monongahela River. And the barge was being shelled, I think you said.

KREIDERMAN: Yes, sir.

FRICK: I suppose there's no chance I would talk to this man. I suppose he's now employed with a Wild West Show.

KREIDERMAN: There were other men began to fire, sir. It got confusing. Men from Pinkertons were killed.

FRICK: I know that Kreiderman. It's a bloody massacre. There are seventy-five dead now and eight thousand soldiers attacking my steel mill.

Exit FRICK and KREIDERMAN. Enter EMMA and MOST.

MOST: What do you want from me?

EMMA: I want you to help us. To help Sasha.

MOST: What kind of help?

EMMA: Money, Hannes, for friendship. As old friends.

MOST: I don't live in the past.

EMMA: For anarchy. For the cause.

MOST: Your companion is drunk with his particular cause, is he not? He feels he is some sort of Messiah. The arrogant Jew will go to Homestead and save us all from the forces of oppression. I beseech you, Emma. I beg you to give up this plan. You see him. You see how his mind works. He is a brainless romantic . . .

EMMA: You'll drink wine with me. When I first came to New York, you took me to Sach's, you ordered wine. Liebfraumilch. The first wine I had ever tasted. You said, "Prosit my young naive lady."

MOST: You are asking me a favour, Emma. Don't remind me of my past mistakes.

EMMA: I was naive.

MOST: So was I.

EMMA: You change drinking wine. I've often noticed it.

MOST: You want me drunk.

EMMA: No, of course not.

MOST: You want me to make a fool of myself.

EMMA: No, Hannes.

MOST: You want money for your lover, Alexander Berkman, so you want me to tell you how much I love you.

EMMA: I want to talk to you. For friendship.

MOST: I will say it. I love you.

EMMA: Hannes . . .

MOST: That means nothing to you, of course. You care about your "work."

EMMA: I care about social justice.

MOST: You delude yourself, Emma. You love attention. You love your life with famous men.

EMMA: Famous men?

MOST: I am the King of the Anarchists. Berkman is a unique personality.

EMMA: I am Emma Goldman.

MOST: How convenient. You have your own fame.

EMMA: We are planning an Attentat.

MOST: You are Berkman's mistress. He sends you out to beg money for his schemes.

MOST exits. EMMA sings.

If the world were fair and fine
I could be a heroine
I could fight the battles
I could win
It's second place in every race
With rules against the way I ran
But reading Russian novels,
Reading Russian novels
I find out I can
Be brave and noble, fine and sure
Self-sacrificing, pure.

Sonja
In *Crime and Punishment*
Became a prostitute
To help her family
Sonja
Agreed to pay that price
Could make that sacrifice
So why not me?

175

If the world were fair and fine
Lightning flashes in the sky
I would change the world
And I would fly
But flying with the wings of man
The victory is bittersweet
Reading Dostoevsky
Reading Dostoevsky
Going on the street
I know I have a heart of gold
I know I'm bought and sold.

>*FRICK enters. EMMA strikes a provocative pose.*
>*She is endearingly naive.*

EMMA: Would you like a good time?
FRICK: With you?
EMMA: Well, yes, of course with me.
FRICK: Would you like me to buy you a drink?
EMMA: All right.
FRICK: At Sach's? The anarchists' cafe?
EMMA: Not there.
FRICK: A young reactionary.
EMMA: Somewhere else. We can walk . . .
FRICK: You don't do this very often.
EMMA: You haven't seen me.
FRICK: I haven't seen you because you haven't been here.
EMMA: I have a natural talent for it.
FRICK: Perhaps.
EMMA: How much I know shouldn't concern you. If I'm willing.
FRICK: I do not give lessons.
EMMA: I know what I'm doing. I know why I'm here. Try me.
FRICK: You look very sweet, my dear. I'm sure you made your dress yourself.
EMMA: And the price is right.
FRICK: Of course it is.
EMMA: If price is a consideration . . .
FRICK: I don't believe you've done this before. You are a seamstress. Some kind of dressmaker. You found yourself short of money so you've gone on the street.
EMMA: I am a courtesan.
FRICK: This is your first night on the street . . .
EMMA: Don't concern yourself with my experience. I'm very experienced.
FRICK: How much money do you need?

EMMA: Ten dollars.
FRICK: Here. Take it.
EMMA: *(A delaying tactic)* You don't want to argue? Over the price?
FRICK: I don't want to discuss it at all.
EMMA: Of course not.
FRICK: You're a professional.
EMMA: Of course.
FRICK: I want you to take the money and go home.
EMMA: Of course . . . go home?
FRICK: I will walk you to your door, young lady, to make sure you are not accosted in this neighbourhood.
EMMA: Thank you.
FRICK: Tell me, young lady, why do you need ten dollars?
EMMA: I have to buy a pistol.
FRICK: *(Urbane)* Oh? And why do you need a pistol?

> *They exit. BERKMAN enters to be met by KREIDERMAN and PARKS, who enter from the opposite side.*

BERKMAN: I want to see Henry Clay Frick.
KREIDERMAN: Whom can I say is calling?
BERKMAN: What?
PARKS: Do you have a card?
BERKMAN: What? Oh, yes. I do.
PARKS: You sell insurance?
KREIDERMAN: That says employment. He's from an employment agency.
BERKMAN: I want to see Henry Clay Frick.
KREIDERMAN: We understand that Mr. . . . I can't read your name.
PARKS: It's Berkman.
KREIDERMAN: But does Mr. Frick want to see you?
BERKMAN: *(He draws his gun)* I want to see your hands up.
KREIDERMAN: Who are you?
BERKMAN: *(Very nervous)* I want to see your hands up . . . I want to see your hands flat on the table . . .
KREIDERMAN: *(Very nervous)* But you want to see Mr. Frick. One of us will have to get Mr. Frick.
BERKMAN: Don't move.
KREIDERMAN: Stay calm. Keep calm. Calm yourself.

> *FRICK enters. He is the only one who seems calm.*

FRICK: *(Behind BERKMAN)* Who are you?

BERKMAN: *(Wheeling to face him)* I want to see your hands up . . . I want your hands flat on the table.
FRICK: *(To KREIDERMAN and PARKS who are moving in)* Get him out of here.
BERKMAN: *(Dodging wildly)* Get back. Get them out of here. Get your hands up. I'm going to shoot. I warned you.
KREIDERMAN: *(Frightened)* How far would you get, friend?
PARKS: Put the gun down, friend . . .
KREIDERMAN: This mill is under armed guard.
PARKS: You wouldn't get out of this office.
KREIDERMAN: You'd never get away with it.

> *FRICK is impatient. He moves towards BERK-MAN. BERKMAN fires wildly. FRICK falls.*

PARKS: *(Grabbing him)* Mr. Frick . . . You've shot Mr. Frick.

> *PARKS tries to pull BERKMAN away. BERKMAN is trying to stab FRICK's legs.*

KREIDERMAN: *(With FRICK)* Are you all right, Mr. Frick?

> *KREIDERMAN helps FRICK offstage. PARKS pulls BERKMAN downstage.*

BERKMAN: You can let go of me, I am not a criminal. I will explain myself.
PARKS: Not on your life, friend. You stay here till the guard gets back.
BERKMAN: This was not a criminal act. This was a political assassination . . .
PARKS: Sure it was. You might have killed the guy . . .
BERKMAN: I've lost my glasses.
PARKS: There's more than that coming to you.
BERKMAN: Can you take my statement?
PARKS: Jesus, statement!
BERKMAN: Will you take this down, please. I want a record of my explanation.
PARKS: You'll hear it in court, friend.

> *EMMA and FEDYA enter the courtroom.*

EMMA: Does it say in the newspapers they'll allow Sasha to have visitors?

FEDYA: It says in the newspapers he is a mad dog. Visiting doesn't seem to be an issue.

EMMA: They must let his family see him.

FEDYA: If he had a family.

EMMA: I can be his sister.

FEDYA: Perhaps.

EMMA: Like Louis Lingg's friend. When Lingg was confined, his friend visited him in prison. They embraced and with the kiss, Lingg received a capsule of nitro-glycerine. I could make a capsule and take it to Sasha. Sasha will want to commit suicide.

FEDYA: Sasha?

EMMA: I don't know why he hasn't killed himself already.

FEDYA: Sasha?

EMMA: He has tried to kill Frick and Frick is still alive. He has been captured by the forces of reaction. His protest is over.

FEDYA: Maybe he's waiting till the newspapers publish his statement.

EMMA: It could be a posthumous statement.

FEDYA: I was joking, Emma.

EMMA: You don't think he wants to live merely to see his statement in the filthy capitalist press.

FEDYA: I don't think he wants to commit suicide.

EMMA: Why not?

FEDYA: Would you?

EMMA: Of course I would. And Sasha would. Any of us would die for what we believed in.

FEDYA: If we had to.

BERKMAN: I have a letter from Emma and Fedya. It is bitter. They say that because Frick did not die, the moral effect of the act will be less. There will not be so much propaganda value. They actually presume to reproach me with my failure to suicide. How am I to kill myself? By banging my head against the bars of my cell? By what right to they reproach me? By the right of revolutionary ethics, I suppose and they are correct. Emma the girl. Fedya the twin. Emma and Fedya will have to forgive me. I did not think that I could live in prison, but I find I must.

> *KREIDERMAN enters, as JUDGE. PARKS escorts BERKMAN to the podium/witness stand on the lower level.*

KREIDERMAN: Is it true that the prisoner wishes to conduct his own defense?

BERKMAN: Yes sir.

KREIDERMAN: *(To PARKS)* He will need an interpreter.

PARKS: Yes sir.
BERKMAN: I . . .
PARKS: I . . .
BERKMAN: . . . address myself to the people.
PARKS: . . . make a speech to all.
BERKMAN: Some may wonder why I have declined a legal defense.
PARKS: Some may think funny I say no to lawyer.
BERKMAN: My reasons are two fold.
PARKS: I say two things.
BERKMAN: In the first place . . .
PARKS: One thing.
BERKMAN: I am an Anarchist.
PARKS: I am an Anarchist.
BERKMAN: I do not believe in man-made law designed to enslave and oppress humanity.
PARKS: I say no lawyer can make up laws made up to tie up and sit down on men.
BERKMAN: Secondly . . .
PARKS: I say two things.
BERKMAN: . . . an extraordinary phenomenon like an Attentat cannot be measured by the narrow standards of legality.
PARKS: A funny thing like an Attentat is not like law.
BERKMAN: It requires a view of the social background to be understood . . .
PARKS: It depends where you come from. What you think.
BERKMAN: The translation is inadequate.
KREIDERMAN: We speak English in this court.
BERKMAN: My English is very poor. But it's good enough to know he's not saying what I'm saying.
EMMA: *(To FEDYA)* I have to speak to Johann Most. He can help us.
KREIDERMAN: Silence in the court.
FEDYA: If he wanted to help he would be here.
KREIDERMAN: There is a disruption in the court.
EMMA: We have to ask him, Fedya. We have to try. Come on.

They exit.

BERKMAN: I have a statement. It's impossible to understand my act against Frick unless you hear the statement.
PARKS: We don't want to know why you did it. We want to see if you did it.
KREIDERMAN: Whatever it is that he's saying, we've heard enough of it.

180

BERKMAN: The removal of a tyrant is not merely justifiable, it is the highest duty of every true revolutionist. Human life is sacred and inviolate. But the killing of a tyrant, of an enemy of the people, is in no way to be considered the taking of a life. In truth, murder and Attentat are to me opposite terms. To remove a tyrant is an act of liberation, the giving of life and opportunity to an oppressed people.

KREIDERMAN: Alexander Berkman. You have been found guilty of the attempted murder of Henry Clay Frick. And the attempted murder of Harry Parks. Of trespassing three times on the property of the Homestead Steel Mills and of trespassing in the office of Henry Clay Frick. I sentence you to twenty-one years in the Western Penitentiary at Pennsylvania.

> *They exit. HELEN enters, followed by EMMA and FEDYA.*

EMMA: I must speak to Johann.

HELEN: He isn't here.

EMMA: I must ask him to help Sasha. They are railroading Sasha into prison.

HELEN: Yes.

EMMA: Have you heard about it, Helen? Sasha in prison. It's dreadful.

HELEN: Go away, Emma.

EMMA: Johann will help us.

HELEN: Go and ask him then.

EMMA: He was our teacher. Of course he'll help.

HELEN: I suppose Sasha thinks that terrorism is part of Hannes' philosophy.

FEDYA: Sasha made his bomb from Hannes' book.

HELEN: You ignore him except when you need him. You make fun of him behind his back. Fedya calls him Johann Sausage, isn't that right?

FEDYA: Sasha's bomb didn't go off. Either Sasha can't make bombs or Johann can't write books.

HELEN: I don't care what you say any more. You can't hurt me, Fedya. Because I'm content.

FEDYA: Because you're smug.

EMMA: We are all anarchists together, are we not? We help each other.

HELEN: I've told you Emma, Johann isn't here.

> *MOST enters and begins to speak to a public meeting. FEDYA and EMMA become part of his audience. HELEN joins him on the platform.*

MOST: The capitalist press cries out against the anarchist. They want our blood. Why? Because someone has made an attempt on the life of Henry Clay Frick. Alexander Berkman waves our banner and hides behind the name of anarchy but he is an inept, self-seeking bungler, with too much faith in a master plan that was ill-timed, ill-formed . . .
EMMA: I demand proof of your insinuations against Alexander Berkman.
MOST: This is a public meeting.
EMMA: Proof.
MOST: These people haven't come here to watch Emma Goldman in temperamental display.
EMMA: They haven't come here to listen to lies.
MOST: I am an anarchist. Alexander Berkman has attempted a murder. He claims that I inspired him . . .
EMMA: Attentat!
MOST: A fool calls me a murderer.
FEDYA: I call you a sausage.
MOST: Berkman was my student. You were all my students. Berkman doesn't learn very well. A young man with a toy pistol and more concern for himself than the worker's problems. Berkman has failed to do anything but find himself the centre of attention.
EMMA: His intention was serious.
MOST: He is a child.
EMMA: It was not a toy gun.
MOST: It was not the gun for the job.
EMMA: It was a cheap revolver. He had no money. Did you give him money? Did you help him at all?
MOST: Of course not.
EMMA: Attentat!
MOST: The Attentat is the act which captures the imagination of men and women everywhere. It makes everyone brave. It makes revolution possible. Has Berkman done this?
FEDYA: Have you?
MOST: Talk to the strikers at Homestead. Berkman tried to "save" those men but they do not understand him. They do not sympathize. They think Frick cheated him in business, perhaps. I have been in prison because of the things I believe in. Berkman makes my philosophy ludicrous.
FEDYA: Berkman is in prison now.
MOST: I denounce him as a self-seeking fool.
EMMA: I call you a coward and a traitor, Johann.
MOST: As you will.
EMMA: You taught me. You called for acts of violence. Sasha is the one of us who moved against the injustice of Homestead.

Sasha acts and you deny everything. Every principle you hold important, you deny.

MOST: You are hysterical.

EMMA: When I met you, you asked me for an ardent friendship. Now you call it hysteria.

MOST: It is hysteria.

EMMA: You do not act. You are impotent.

MOST: I do not think of anarchy as some kind of springtime sexual rite.

FEDYA: Johann Wurst. Johann Sausage.

MOST: Berkman's mistress attacks me in the columns of my own newspaper. Because I talk about his stupidity. Because I tell the truth. Berkman was arrogant, opportunistic.

EMMA: Stop it, Johann!

MOST: Egotistical, pretentious.

EMMA: Stop it!

MOST: Self-indulgent.

>*EMMA takes off her belt. She rushes at MOST. The belt comes down on his back.*

EMMA: Be bold. Be arrogant. I am sure you will be brave.

MOST: Emma!

EMMA: Who is not with me is against me!

MOST: Emma!

EMMA: I think for myself. I speak for myself, Johann!

>*EMMA is exhausted. There is a long pause. Though it may not be possible to arrange exits, EMMA and FEDYA are alone.*

FEDYA: Anarchy is a glorious political theory. We have proved it doesn't work.

EMMA: No.

FEDYA: We said an act against a tyrant would begin the revolution. We found we were wrong. We said that man was pure and fine . . .

EMMA: Man is pure and fine.

FEDYA: You are.

EMMA: I believe in freedom, the right to self-expression. Everyone's right to beautiful, radiant things.

FEDYA: You are pure and fine and gullible.

EMMA: *(Sings)*

I know I can show you wonders
I can paint the flags I fly

I know dreamers can build castles
I know castles can have banners
I know dreams are going to flash across the sky.

There are no countries
There are no kings
Only the people and all they can wish for
All of the beautiful radiant things.

I know I will do my living
In my future not your past
There are certain stirring speeches
There are drumbeats every morning
And the chance that things will start to move too fast.

There are no countries
There are no kings
Only the people and all they can wish for
All of the beautiful radiant things.

Blackout.